poverty
a mission study

Edited by Jack A. Keller Jr.

Poverty: A Mission Study edited by Jack A. Keller Jr. © 2012 Women's Division, the General Board of Global Ministries, The United Methodist Church. All rights reserved.

No part of this book may be reproduced or transmitted in any form or by any means, electronic or mechanical, including photocopying or recording, or by means of any information storage or retrieval system, except as may be expressly permitted by the 1976 Copyright Act or in writing from the publisher. Requests for permission should be addressed in writing to:

Director of Mission Education and Enrichment
Women's Division, the General Board of Global Ministries
The United Methodist Church
475 Riverside Drive, Room 1504
New York, NY 10115
Fax: (212) 870-3695
Phone: (212) 870-3745

Photos by Paul Jeffrey appear by courtesy of the photographer.

All biblical quotations, unless otherwise noted, are from the New Revised Standard Version (NRSV) of the Bible, copyright © 1989, by the Division of Christian Education of the National Council of the Churches of Christ in the United States of America. Used by permission. All rights reserved.

All quotes from *The Book of Discipline of The United Methodist Church*—2008 copyright © 2008 by The United Methodist Publishing House. Used by permission.

All quotes from *The Book of Resolutions of The United Methodist Church*—2008 copyright © 2008 by The United Methodist Publishing House. Used by permission.

ISBN: 978-0-9848176-1-0
Library of Congress Control Number: 2011944873

Cover design: Emily Miller
Cover image by Fuse/Gettyimages.com
Design: Nanako Inoue

Printed in the United States of America.

Table of Contents

Introduction

Chapter 1. Are We Avoiding or Encountering the Poor? Stories of United Methodist Work with the Poor 7
Denise Johnson Stovall

Chapter 2. The Bible and the Poor 17
Jack A. Keller Jr.

Chapter 3. Our United Methodist Heritage 29
Kenneth L. Carder

Chapter 4. Poverties in the United States 41
Pamela D. Couture

Chapter 5. Global Poverty: We're All Connected 53
David Wildman

Chapter 6. Helping the Global Poor Have a Working Chance 65
Elizabeth Calvin

Chapter 7. Consumerism and Spiritual Poverty 79
Paul L. Escamilla

Chapter 8. Charity Is Not Enough 91
Sung-ok Lee

Conclusion 105

Bibliography 109

About the Editor 115

Contributors 115

Hilmia Dipru bathes at the well in the temporary village of Kavitikuda, Sri Lanka. Several families from this settlement are about to move into new permanent homes sponsored by the YMCA, with support from ACT International. *(Paul Jeffrey)*

Introduction

The biblical message of salvation is both a comfort and a promise to the poor and, at the same time, a call to those who are not materially poor to be connected with God's vision of shalom for all. Standing with the poor is a matter of learning a new vocabulary of values. Instead of using the world's vocabulary to label the poor—as failures, as lazy, as unimportant, as not having anything to offer, as "them"—Christians use a vocabulary of love. Persons who are poor are our sisters and brothers, created by God and redeemed by Jesus Christ. John Westerhoff, former professor of theology and Christian nurture at Duke University, once said that we should go down the street imagining that angels are flying in front of every person we meet (including every poor person, we might add), shouting: "Make way for the image of God! Make way for the image of God!"

Our Christian faith invites each of us to become agents of God's compassion and healing in a wounded world. The capacity for compassion, *feeling with* the other person, makes all the difference. Christian traditions of social outreach and social justice are grounded in the human capacity to "feel with" the pains, sorrows, and frustrations of those who suffer.

This study is designed to help participants recognize and claim for themselves the connections among Scripture, church tradition (especially the Wesleyan and United Methodist streams of that tradition), compassion for the poor, social outreach, and social justice.

While information by itself is not sufficient for faithful living, information is necessary. The counsel of the great Jewish thinker Martin Buber is instructive in this regard: "The graver the crisis becomes the more earnest and consciously responsible is the knowledge demanded of us; for although what is demanded is a deed, only that deed which is born of knowledge will help to overcome the crisis."[1]

We need a clear picture of what the world looks like and why it is the way it is. That means we need to be informed by the best sociological, economic, and political analyses available. This study will provide participants with information about the reality of impoverished communities domestically and globally, with special attention to women and children; the root causes of domestic and global poverty; and possible strategies to alleviate poverty.

Our perceptions of and willingness to respond to poverty go beyond mere information, of course. What we see, feel, and do will ultimately be reflections of whether our hearts and minds are touched by the lived realities of poverty. While statistics and patterns and trends are important, they should never obscure the human faces and voices they represent. Throughout this study, therefore, we will use a two-focus lens, so to speak, giving prominence whenever possible to stories of particular persons and communities as a way of making the overview reported by statistics and theoretical analysis concrete and compelling.

Chapter 1

What stereotypes do many of us have about the poor? Where do those assumptions come from? How do they make us feel? How do they influence our actions? What are poor people really like? How would we know? How might we go about finding out? Can we learn to listen carefully to the experiential experts, the ones who know firsthand what it means to be poor?

In our opening chapter, "Are We Avoiding or Encountering the Poor?" Denise Johnson Stovall helps us begin to answer those questions by telling us stories about United Methodists involved in ministry with the poor who actually encounter the poor. Some of the encounters happen in the trenches, so to speak, and others happen at the periphery. Some people have been at this for a long while, and others are just beginning. It's not a matter of one size fits all; rather, it's a matter of taking one step forward from wherever you are now.

Chapter 2

Characteristic of all strands of the biblical tradition is a concern for the poor and vulnerable. In fact, according to Scripture, the measure of the moral and spiritual health of an entire community is precisely its treatment of marginal groups and individuals. In Chapter 2, "The Bible and the Poor," Jack A. Keller Jr. examines selected, representative passages from the Torah, the Psalms, the Prophets, Gospels, Acts, and New Testament letters in terms of three major themes related to the poor. What, according to Scripture, is the fundamental basis of human worth and dignity? What does the Bible say about God's concern and compassion for the poor as important members of the community? And who is responsible for the well-being of the poor and the vulnerable?

Chapter 3

In Chapter 3, "Our United Methodist Heritage," Kenneth L. Carder helps us see that "God's preferential option for the poor" has deep roots in the life and ministry of John Wesley. Wesley regarded the poor as more than a mission field, as more than recipients of benevolence. Poor people are valued members of a community.

Wesley created numerous institutions to address the systemic needs of the poor, and he spoke out forcefully against exploitative practices of all sorts. His advocacy for the marginalized was grounded not only in scriptural mandates but in direct, personal knowledge of poor people and their struggles.

Poor people remained important to Methodists in nineteenth and twentieth century America, but this concern found expression more in mission programs and institutions and less in direct participation of the poor in the churches. Ministry to the poor tended to be seen as the responsibility of select groups and agencies. Happily, we have seen in the past two decades a recovery among United Methodists of renewed *presence* and ministry *with* the poor.

Chapter 4

In Chapter 4, "Poverties in the United States," Pamela D. Couture begins by helping us to consider the difference between a church *for* the poor and a church *of* the poor—and to recognize the existence of both in The United Methodist Church. She goes on to recount briefly some of the responses in American history to the question "Who is responsible for eradicating poverty?" giving special attention to federal policies in recent decades that profoundly affect women and children who experience poverty.

Drawing on extensive social scientific research, Couture describes the scope and character of poverty in this country, especially among women and children. The descriptive patterns she identifies suggest possible

Children do their school homework in the mountainous community of Foret-des-Pins, Haiti. *(Paul Jeffrey)*

directions for response, both at the level of governmental policy and at the level of action by United Methodist Women in congregations and annual conferences.

Chapter 5

In Chapter 5, "Global Poverty," David Wildman helps us look carefully and critically at the global economic system that drains life and resources out of communities around the globe to serve the consumptive culture of the wealthy. Six case studies (sweatshop conditions in the garment industry in Bangladesh, poverty and child labor in Uzbekistan, small farmers versus agribusiness in Haiti, conflict minerals and cell phones in the Democratic Republic of the Congo, climate change devastation in the Pacific Islands and elsewhere, and U.S. militarism in Afghanistan) allow us to see the particular challenges impoverished communities are facing and what those on the front lines are doing to claim their own dignity and basic rights.

Chapter 6

In Chapter 6, "Helping the Global Poor Have a Working Chance," Elizabeth Calvin explores the general features and benefits of two relatively small-scale but fast-growing strategies for alleviating poverty in less developed countries: fair trade and microfinance. The fair trade movement involves organizations that promote markets in highly developed countries for goods produced, usually on a small scale, in less developed countries and to do so in ways that maximize the fair return to the originating farmer or artisan. The microfinance movement consists of many organizations that encourage small-scale entrepreneurship in less developed countries by providing small amounts of investment capital outside conventional banking channels.

While neither strategy involves women exclusively, women have been major participants and beneficiaries of both, and some of the organizations involved in both strategies are focused exclusively on women. United Methodist Women has been an early and continuing supporter of specific efforts of both strategies.

Chapter 7

"Getting and spending," if that is all we do and all we are, truly does, as Wordsworth says, "lay waste our powers." In Chapter 7, "Consumerism and Spiritual Poverty," Paul L. Escamilla reminds us that while we as human beings are to some degree inescapably consumers, we as Christians cannot be reduced to that economic moniker. All human beings need and deserve a certain measure of the good gifts of God's creation, so "the choice is not whether to be on or off the consumption grid but how deeply enmeshed in that grid we allow ourselves to become."

Escamilla suggests that we take our cues about consumption from God, who "has a modest aspect, needing little and offering much. Since we are made in God's image, we, too, are fashioned for modesty, for choosing enough over more, adequacy over excess, restraint over extravagance." We need our "consuming interests" to be genuinely worthy of the lives we spend on them.

Chapter 8

Chapter 1 of this book asks the question "Are we avoiding or encountering the poor?" Chapter 8, "Charity Is Not Enough," asks a parallel question: Are we avoiding or encountering the root causes of poverty? Dealing with the root causes of poverty requires looking beyond symptoms of poverty for the systemic structures that keep people in poverty, going beyond charity to work for *justice*.

Sung-ok Lee provides in this chapter a helpful, detailed review of the impressive track record in recent decades of United Methodist Women in partnership with other organizations in the struggle for justice for poor people in the United States and around the world, especially for women and children. She helps us see the importance of (1) careful observation and description of any problematic situation, (2) critical analysis of how power is wielded in that situation, and (3) imaginative and organized responses that help change the structures that contribute to the problem.

Taken together, these chapters are meant to engage our hearts and our heads and our hands. We'll explore, first of all, the reasons of the heart that call us to be in ministry with the poor. We'll recover and reclaim the stories and values that shape us, that tell us what God is like and who we are. This study recognizes, second, that to be in ministry with the poor we need to understand what is really going on in our towns and around the world. We need to learn who is hurting and why they are hurting. Finally, this study is an invitation to discover what we can do as agents of compassion, healing, and transformation. What will we do to make God's love incarnate in our actions?

Note

1. Martin Buber, *Paths in Utopia*, translated by R. F. C. Hull (New York: Macmillan, 1950), 129.

A homeless woman in Seattle. *(Paul Jeffrey)*

Chapter 1

Are We Avoiding or Encountering the Poor?
Stories of United Methodist Work with the Poor

Denise Johnson Stovall

Being with the Poor is Love

"The United Methodist Church should be showing real love through ministries with the poor," said the Rev. Dr. Joseph Echols Lowery, pastor emeritus of Cascade United Methodist Church in Atlanta, Georgia. "Jesus said we will always have the poor, but how we treat them is what matters," Lowery said. "We shouldn't be treating them in a way we wouldn't want to be treated."

An icon of the civil rights movement, Lowery is past national president of the Southern Christian Leadership Conference (SCLC). He co-founded the organization with the Rev. Dr. Martin Luther King Jr. in 1957. King was the first president, and Lowery was the third president. Although he is retired as a pastor in The United Methodist Church, persons still seek his advice and request him to preach during special occasions. In 2008, Lowery was asked by President Barack Obama to give the benediction during President Obama's 2009 inauguration.

In an interview for this chapter, Lowery reflected on how many people do not consider doing ministries with the poor. "What they are really doing is 'charity,'" he said. "In early versions of the Bible, 1 Corinthians 13:13 said, 'The greatest of these is *charity*.' But now it says *love*. That's because theologians realized being like Christ is sharing God's love. So being with the poor is *love*."

Lowery contends that the new millennium has the rich accepting much too casually a new type of poor—the working poor. "We will always have the poor among us. But we have not addressed the working poor," the pastor continued. "These are the people not making enough money to live."

Jesus Calls Us to This Work

Bishop Minerva G. Carcaño, episcopal leader of the Phoenix Area of The United Methodist Church, is also an advocate for the poor, immigrants and disenfranchised people in our midst. In her book *I Believe in Jesus* she describes growing up in "great poverty" as a daughter of laborers who picked cotton in the Rio Grande Valley on the Texas–Mexico border: "Living in a region of great economic disparity where the minority of white persons owned most of the land, and the majority Hispanic population worked in the the fields, racism and classism afflicted our lives like a wound that never heals," she said. "Working with and in behalf of the poor is fundamental work for all who profess the name of Christ Jesus as Lord and

Savior. Jesus himself calls us to this work as necessary for the building of God's own reign."[1]

Founded on Practicing Ministry *with* the Poor

The Rev. Judi Hoffman, co-pastor of Edgehill United Methodist Church in Nashville, Tennessee, said her church has been "practicing ministry *with* the poor" since the founding of this congregation in 1966. It was started by the Rev. Bill Barnes and a handful of faithful neighbors. "We offer meals, provide emergency assistance and shelter to some of the ones who don't have a roof over their heads. Over the years we have tutored children, served the older adults, and provided food boxes," Hoffman said. She continued,

> The signature ministry is Brighter Days, an after-school program for children as well as a summer day camp. Nancy Crutcher is the director of this ministry, which serves more than thirty children every day. More recently, the congregation purchased a house and started "Parent Place," a ministry with teen parents. Five young adults have formed an intentional community, living a block from the church. They also have committed two years to service in the neighborhood. Our Free Store provides household items at no cost for those in need. All aspects of the ministry are team led.

Choir Youth Are Ambassadors of Christ

In 1990 a small group of youth and adults at Christ Church United Methodist in Louisville, Kentucky, went on that congregation's first high school choir tour. They headed to the beach, with concerts in prisons, churches, and retirement homes along the way. In 1992, thirty-six members of this growing choir went on tour. The first trip was to Harrisburg, Pennsylvania, where they presented a three-day Bible school to inner-city children in the area of Park Street United Methodist Church and Fourth United Church of Christ. The choir and alumni groups returned to that destination for nine trips.

"Youth experienced the presence of Christ through the lives of those children," said Dan Stokes, director of music ministries at Christ Church. "We've been to more than twelve states over the years. The choir size has changed, destinations have changed, but the constant throughout the years has been mission and service to others as our focus."

Recent tours have opened the door for service with two hundred Vietnam veterans in Asheville, North Carolina, where fifty-five youth ate, worked, and sang side by side with the men for three grace-filled days.

Stokes gives thanks that many choir alumni have answered the call to service throughout the community and the world. Among them are the following:

- Holly Steward is a missionary in Zambia running a school for orphan children.
- Eric Yff is in Malawi with the Peace Corps.
- Sarah Ruzic was a missionary in Guatemala and just finished a three-year stint with Teach for America in Houston.
- Logan Mast has done medical missions to Honduras.
- Matt Walton is pursuing a master's degree in social work and plans a career in drug and alcohol rehabilitation.
- Ben Monsma is an AmeriCorps construction assistant with Habitat for Humanity.
- Ben Williams and Chris Horan work in urban schools in Louisville while also stepping forward as the new generation of directors for this choir and the handbell ringers.

- Susan West is a houseparent at a residential facility for adults with developmental disabilities.
- Lesley Gookin is assistant treasurer for the Kentucky Annual Conference of The United Methodist Church and just returned from a mission trip to Honduras.

"Most importantly, we give thanks for the privilege of serving in the name of the Risen Christ," Stokes said.

"And a Child Shall Lead Them"

Members of Highland Park United Methodist Church in Dallas, Texas, are witnesses to the verse "And a child shall lead them." Eleven-year-old Grace Nobles has been educating her classmates on being in mission with the poor. "Grace has collected soccer balls and basketballs, clothing, and school equipment for the forty-five orphans at Christian Praise Children's Home in the Philippines," Stephen Raynor of Highland Park United Methodist's mission ministry said with pride. "With support from her parents [Bruce Nobles and wife Kathy Koorenny], Grace has filled several boxes weighing fifty pounds each with needed items. The Nobles family has also raised money for a new projector to help the orphans learn hymns in English."

The mission of the children's home is "to help improve the quality of life of the neglected children by providing programs and services. All neglected children will achieve dignity, self-esteem, and self-sufficiency through residential care."[2] Teachers at Christian Praise Children's Home say they offer the compassion and love that gives the children an opportunity to have a clean, honest life through creating an environment that educates and helps them develop integrity and dignity. "The poverty in the Philippines," said Raynor, "like that of India or parts of Mexico or even in Russia, can be a crushing poverty, like the two children of a woman whose husband severely beat her so she moved in with a schoolteacher in Cebu who made about two hundred dollars per month. Those children had the clothes on their back and beautiful smiles and seemed very bright, but without some kind of intervention, the chance that they can ever go to college is zero. Just looking into the eyes of their mother, you see the sense of hopelessness."

Did Raynor have any stereotypes of Filipinos before his first mission trip?

I had a stereotype of the street children who are often forced by parents or circumstances to beg on the streets, thinking of them as thieves, fakers, lazy, or drug addicts not worthy of giving even a dime to. However, in working with Child and Family Services in Baguio, Philippines, and through The United Methodist Church Central District of Manila, Bishop Toquero's office, I learned that street children number at least seventy-seven thousand in Manila. Right in front of Central Methodist Church in Manila, I observed and listened to street children in a nonresidential program who were as young as three years old.

Raynor discovered that most of the children are decent, but circumstances have either corrupted them as a necessity to stay alive or someone beats them in order to have them earn an income. Most street children are unable to attend school.

I suppose I learned that the street children are beautiful children of God who never had the opportunity to grow up in a well-adjusted household with two parents who love them. . . . In spite of their petty theft for which the Republic of the Philippines oftentimes houses

In the Philippines, the government estimated that there were at least 22 thousand street children nationwide. UNICEF estimated that there were approximately 250 thousand street children. Welfare officials believed that the number increased as a result of widespread unemployment in rural areas. Many street children appeared to be abandoned and engaged in scavenging or begging.

(U.S. Department of State, "2005 Country Reports on Human Rights Practices: Philippines," March 8, 2006, www.state.gov/g/drl/rls/hrrpt/2005/61624.htm)

ten-year-old children with adults charged with serious crimes, the children do not deserve incarceration. And that those prisons are worse than the quarantine shelter my dog went through in Hawaii.

Raynor said many of the wealthiest citizens of Manila do not believe in charity. "Don't give that child a peso," said a friend who was appointed by the president of the Philippines to travel to Saudi Arabia on business. Raynor continued,

> Through Highland Park United Methodist we avoid giving money but instead want to give the gift through the Holy Spirit of strengthening church ministries and education for children at risk. For each child we touch through the dignity of providing to him or her a school uniform, and perhaps providing school supplies, books, and access to the world through a computer, we are keeping that child away from dark alleys with men who may abuse or hurt him or her. We are keeping that child away from glue sniffing. We are providing help from God toward training the child to help others perhaps through a career in teaching or nursing. We are making the child's world a better place as he or she learns to love others through the Holy Spirit.

Church and Community Worker Was the Answer

If you think a former United Methodist Women national officer looks forward to retiring from being an advocate for poor women, children, and youth, you're wrong! Josephine Deere, a former national secretary and a member of the Oklahoma Indian Missionary Conference, is always happy to describe the ministries with the poor in her area:

> Let me share with you our ministry at Clinton Indian Church and Community Center [CICCC]. "This ministry is located in the heart of the Cheyenne and Arapaho Nation and in an area of the state where income levels are very low. At one time the church was going pretty strong, but attendance fell and it began to struggle. It was noticed there were a lot of children around the church. The pastor who had a two-point charge that included Clinton had a couple adults and several children who would attend. In discussion with the adults,

it was obvious there needed to be some type of children's ministry in that area. The church and the housing addition that houses a lot of the native people in that area are on the west side of town while the tribal facilities are on the east side of town. A number of activities would take place at the tribal facilities, but with no transportation, these children were getting left out. A lot of the children in this area are being raised by grandparents who live on social security or a very low fixed income. We, the Oklahoma Indian Missionary Conference, were able to have one of our own become a church and community worker and be appointed to Clinton. The program is starting to grow, and the children are a blessing to all who come in contact with them.

Deere reports that the center is still struggling for funds. "The CICCC is the first established center for our conference. Also a number of the children are direct descendents of some of the Cheyenne and Arapaho who were massacred in the Sand Creek Massacre that Chivington lead, and those memories run deep."

Poor Christians Who Take Their Faith Seriously

When you visit Sixty-first Avenue United Methodist Church in Nashville, you will be warmly greeted and will receive resource material that reads, "Sixty-first Avenue United Methodist Church invites you to become a part of our faith community. Together, we seek to follow Christ in the Nations Neighborhood, sharing God's love and sowing seeds of hope!" The sentiment may not be unusual, but the times for worship and church school are not like a typical United Methodist Church. The weekly worship is at six o'clock every Saturday night, and church school is held Saturdays at 4:45 p.m. to 6:45 p.m.

The Rev. Paul Slentz reflected on his ministry at Sixty-first Avenue United Methodist:

> Over my fourteen years at Sixty-first Avenue United Methodist Church, I have grown to know and love the members of this small congregation of about eighty in Nashville. [It is] made up almost entirely of individuals and families with incomes under the official poverty lines [including many homeless individuals] . . . poor Christians who take their faith seriously [and] are in ministry daily. This often takes the form of acts of compassion for one another—sharing food, shelter, and kindness with those who at any particular point in their lives might be penniless. But it also takes the form of reaching out to others in the wider community.

Slentz gave an example of low-income members of the congregation who are very active in hosting a Last Minute Toy Store at the church. The store provides toys for more than 4,500 children.

> The point I would make is that being given the opportunity to serve, being given encouragement and support to practice love of neighbor, is as important to members of our congregation as receiving material assistance. To always be on the receiving end of charity is deadly to the spirit. To be given a chance to help others gives dignity and purpose.

The pastor told the story of an older church member who has some mental limitations and lives in pretty rough circumstances. She calls daily to ask if she can come and help out with something at the church. "She desires to serve her Lord daily and it lifts her spirits to be able to do something, even if it's no more than straightening up the clothing closet," he said.

The final point I would want to make is that in our setting the "connection" with more affluent congregations enables ministry by the low-income members of my congregation. For those wealthier congregations this takes three forms: "doing for" (giving financial and in-kind gifts to keep the bills paid and ministries funded), "doing with" (working side by side in ministry with members of our congregation, and "being with" (just being in relationship as fellow brothers and sisters in Christ, worshipping God as brothers and sisters desiring to praise God and seeking the gift of healing). I have come to believe that all three levels of engagement are essential for partnership between affluent congregations and poor congregations.

Practice What You Preach— in Prison

Members of Christ United Methodist Church in Franklin, Tennessee, have been teaching the *Disciple* Bible study series in a maximum-security prison for years. Christ United Methodist provides former inmates with clothing, one thousand dollars when persons are released, a connection with an employment agency, and friendship. A dozen ex-inmates now worship at the church. Jerry Nail and Harry Boyko began the ministry of teaching *Disciple* in the Riverbend Maximum Security Institution in Nashville.

In 2001 the story of Bible study ministry in the prisons of North Carolina was shared with a group of men meeting as they normally did at Christ United Methodist on a Wednesday morning. One person in the group, Nail, who had been in four different *Disciple* studies, heard God's call to become part of such a ministry in Tennessee. He had been open to God's leading for several years but nothing seemed to fit. This did.

After almost a year of talking to the director of the North Carolina Bible study ministry and contacting administrative personnel in Tennessee prisons, he finally got to talk with the chaplain at Riverbend Maximum Security Institution in Nashville. With the door finally open, Nail and Boyko met with the first class of approximately twelve inmates in the fall of 2002. As leaders they soon discovered that, as with all *Disciple* Bible study groups, it was a growing experience for them just as it was for the inmates. Classes have been held on the various *Disciple* Bible study modules each year since.

After two years of *Disciple* Bible studies, the inmates requested a Sunday morning communion service because of what they experienced at communion together at the end of the *Disciple* Bible studies. This service on Sunday mornings at eight o'clock has grown. Now the prison chapel is full on Sunday mornings. Retired pastors, church staff, and pastors of churches in the community rotate as officiates at the table. Sunday after Sunday Nail and Boyko are there, along with visitors who are part of the programs that have grown out of the relationships that have been established. Inmates look forward to seeing their "pen pal" who corresponds with them on a regular basis, a program coordinated by another volunteer. There is also a visitation ministry with those in the areas of the prison that are more secure. Each of these ministries has opened participants' eyes to the importance of sharing with an inmate who needs to know someone cares enough to share God's love in concrete ways.

This ministry continues to grow. As inmates are paroled or fulfill the terms of their incarceration they need help in transitioning into society, especially with the stigma so many attach to those who have been incarcerated. A group called "Building Lives" was formed and incorporated to develop ministries that include recruiting, training, and deploying mentors to work with ex-inmates to secure housing and support the ex-inmates in the transition time as they seek employment, to help with employment, to get drivers licenses and social services that are needed, and when possible to help get vehicles that enable the ex-immates to get to work. Volunteers are amazed at how much they learn about the difficulties and the prejudices those who have been incarcerated must deal with as they seek the new life to which they have been introduced while in prison. This ministry provides important support for those who want to find a new life that is grounded in God's love and their love for all of God's children.

The Rev. Mark Price, minister of spiritual formation at Christ United Methodist and a veteran teacher of *Disciple* Bible studies at Riverbend, sums it up this way: "We have discovered that we are sisters and brothers in Christ who share a common journey and a love that extends to all. As God's love and grace become incarnate in our relationships with inmates and ex-inmates, we come to see with eyes that have the lens of past prejudices removed so we can see as God sees our sister and brother."

"We Love You, and There Is Nothing You Can Do About It!"

The website for St. John's United Methodist Church in Houston, Texas, better known as St. John's Downtown, says it all: "You are invited to experience the power of unconditional love at 8:00 a.m., 10:00 a.m., and 12 noon. We love you, and there is nothing you can do about it!"

In 1992 the Rev. Kirbyjon Caldwell, pastor of Windsor Village United Methodist Church, Houston, asked two faithful lay members, Rudy and Juanita Rasmus, to attend St. John's United Methodist Church in downtown Houston to revive the struggling congregation. Beginning with nine existing members in 1992, St. John's Downtown has grown to more than nine thousand members. "The church is one of the most culturally diverse congregations in the country," Mr. Rasmus contends. "Every week people of every social and economic background share the same pew. We have a very inclusive community that includes people from 175 zip codes and many who live outdoors."

Mr. and Ms. Rasmus, pastors at the church, attribute the success of the church to a compassionate congregation that has embraced the vision of tearing down the walls of classism, sexism, and racism and building bridges of unconditional love. The church is known for its infectious hope that God will change lives. The congregation is composed of one-third affluent members, such as multimillionaire entertainer Beyonce Knowles, the Knowles family, and recording artist Kelly Rowland; one-third middle income members; and one-third either homeless or formerly homeless persons.

To meet the physical needs of the community, Mr. Rasmus co-founded Bread of Life Inc., a not-for-profit corporation, in December of 1992 and began serving dinners to the homeless in the sanctuary at St. John's. Today, Bread of Life has become a lighthouse of love providing an array of services to homeless men and women, seven days a week, in the recently constructed Daybreak Community Health Facility on the St. John's campus. Bread of Life currently provides more than fourteen thousand hot meals and eighty thousand pounds of fresh food each month to hungry and homeless individuals. On a daily basis, the agency also provides job training and placement, substance abuse and psychiatric counseling, and HIV testing, prevention, and education. Every night two hundred homeless men and women sleep in the campus gymnasium, which converts to the After-Dark Program from six o'clock at night to seven o'clock in the morning, seven days a week.

In the aftermath of Hurricane Katrina in 2005, efforts were begun to construct housing for low-income persons. The Knowles-Temenos Place Apartment Complex is now open and includes forty-three single-occupancy units designed to provide transitional living accommodations for women and men who are taking significant steps in improving their lives. "We are intentionally counterculture—counter-church-culture, that is," Mr. Rasmus said. "We aren't trying to be different just to be different. I wanted to touch the people nobody else was touching, so I was fiercely committed to making them feel comfortable."

The Rasmuses say they promote diversity by economic status, marital status, race and ethnicity, age, sexual orientation, and every other conceivable group of people. "We actively invite them all," Mr. Rasmus said, continuing,

> We defend each person's right to come to church. From time to time, an enfranchised person comes to me to complain about the addicts or homeless people. In those conversations, I am the champion of the underdog. I try not to use the same language Jesus used when he defended the common people against the self-righteous condemnation of the "group that's always right," but I let them know that the people they are complaining about are my honored guests—no question about it. It's interesting that the addicts and homeless people never complain about the self-righteous attitudes of some enfranchised people. I haven't figured out the reason for that yet, but it's true.

Mr. Rasmus explained that sometimes those who were once struggling are now the ones complaining about those still struggling. "After a few months, they can't remember what it was like to be a lying, stealing, manipulative, irresponsible addict, and they are quick to condemn people who are still struggling." When asked what he is going to do about the homeless folk, the addicts, the outcasts, he responds:

> You need to show them the same unconditional love and grace we showed you when you were smoking crack and sitting in the pew week after week—for years! You didn't have anywhere to go, and we took you in. That gay guy doesn't have a church to go to because he feels condemned everywhere he goes, and we're going to show him some love. Figuratively and literally, we touch people in all kinds of ways. At St. John's, it starts in the parking lot when our "ambassadors" reach out to shake people's hands. In the worship service, we hug people. To be honest, it startles some people when an addict or a homeless person hugs them the first Sunday they come to church here. It's a part of our culture of caring, and it communicates the warmth in God's kingdom. Some people, it's true, don't feel comfortable, and they withdraw from being hugged. If they'll stick around, they might find that their walls come down and the hugs touch them more deeply than they ever imagined.

A Voice for the Least of These

Petrella Booker, a member of Hamilton Park United Methodist Church, Dallas, is also the coordinator for the North Texas Annual Conference. "I became the Executive Director for the Dallas Bethlehem Center [DBC] in July 2009," she explained. "The DBC is a national mission institution owned by United Methodist Women. I guess the Lord chose me because he knows I am a heart person and I never give up once committed. I am very clear about one thing—just because working poor families have less financially does not mean their children should lack in opportunities to learn."

"Our goal at the Bethlehem Center is not only to close the achievement gap but to surpass the expectations of the naysayers. It's a shame that systems once designed to help build bridges out of poverty are now being torn to shreds bit by bit," she said. "I will continue to be a voice for the least of these, our children, our future, our hope, our precious resources. I pray that I am not the only one. Let us continue to educate policymakers about the long-term benefits of early child development programs, invest in teachers and job readiness programs for underemployed and disenfranchised persons."

The Suitcase Ministry

Members of the United Methodist Church of Green Trails in Chesterfield, Missouri, developed a ministry with children in poverty who needed suitcases for moving to and from foster care homes by providing new luggage sets. Under the leadership of the Rev. Nathanael Berneking, senior pastor, the church donated sixty-eight brand new suitcase sets in three weeks. "The Missouri Alliance for Children and Families was very happy to receive these donations on behalf of foster children," said Jerry Ruth Williams, a former elected director of the Women's Division of the United Methodist General Board of Global Ministries. "Most of the time the children place their belongings in plastic trash bags. It would be wonderful if more United Methodist Women members could do this [project]. New suitcases provide a heightened sense of dignity and hope for these children. This project is only one of the ways the people of Green Trails demonstrate 'extravagant generosity' toward others," she said.

> Let each of us commit to reaching out and caring for children in the way God calls us, whether it is to wipe a tear, bandage a scraped knee, comfort a scraped heart, tutor a struggling student, paint over graffiti, provide an internship, coach a sports team, or give a child a hand. With God, it is never too late for us. God offers us fresh beginnings every day, the chance to find the new start needed, the opportunity to provide a new start for a child. Thanks be to God. Amen.
>
> (Children's Defense Fund, 2000 National Observance of Children's Sabbaths Manual, Washington, DC: Children's Defense Fund, 2000)

NOTES

1. Minerva G. Carcaño, *I Believe in Jesus* (New York: Women's Division, The General Board of Global Ministries, The United Methodist Church, 2008).
2. Christian Praise Children's Home, "Our Mission/Vision," www.christianpraisechildrenshome.org.

Beatriz Sousa da Silva, a 6-year-old girl in the Esperança Sustainable Development Project, in front of her family's house. Her family is part of a pioneering jungle community in the Amazonian jungles of Brazil.
(Paul Jeffrey)

Chapter 2

The Bible and the Poor

Jack A. Keller Jr.

Who cares about poor people? Why should we care? We live in a meritocracy, some Americans would claim, in which those with talent, good judgment, and a solid work ethic are rewarded financially and deserve to enjoy all the goods and services and experiences money can buy. The myth of "rugged individualism" is convenient for those of us who enjoy a materially comfortable lifestyle. We've earned what we have, after all, so we can do as we like with that bounty. It is unfortunate, of course, that some people live in poverty, but why should that be our concern? If we perceive our communities as merely a collection of individuals, instead of individuals-inextricably-in-community, and we are one of the privileged individuals, then there is a kind of logic to our indifference to the poor. But it is not a logic informed by the biblical witness.

Created and Redeemed by God

The Bible presents a sharply different understanding in which (1) each and every individual is extraordinarily valuable and (2) individuals can flourish only by participating in communities, and communities can be healthy only if all of their members are full participants. Let's look briefly, first, at what Scripture has to say about the fundamental basis of human worth and dignity. Then we will explore in more detail what the Bible has to say about life in community.

The first creation story mentioned in Genesis (1:1 to 2:3), and especially Genesis 1:26–27, provides an important clue about why human beings are so valuable. What is the significance of being made in the image of God?

While a "substantialist" understanding was popular in earlier centuries, recent scholarship has favored a holistic and "relational" understanding. According to the substantialist view, the image of God in us is embodied in some attribute, substance, or endowment, such as reason, will, freedom, or creativity. The relational view, in contrast, holds that "image" refers to the entire human self, not to a particular part.

An analogy from the ancient world may help us grasp what is meant by being in the image of God. Monarchs who ruled over vast empires would typically erect images or statues of themselves across the land to signify the scope of their royal authority. Likewise, human beings are to be God's image on earth, representing divine dominion over all creation. But human beings are not inert statues; God has delegated to humanity both power and responsibility (Genesis 1:28). The purpose of this power-sharing relationship with God is to foster a right relationship between human beings and the rest of the creatures of the world. The authority God delegates to us is not license for exploitation but responsibility for caregiving.[1]

Notice one more feature of the first account of creation. After God has created human beings and given them their unique marching orders, God declares that these creatures—in fact, all creatures—are "very good" (Genesis 1:31). Human beings are valued by God, appreciated by God, loved by God.

There is no mention yet in Genesis of any basis for human worth other than being created in the divine image and being treasured by God. There is no mention of social privilege given to some and denied to others or any corresponding hierarchy of value. Rather the implication is that all human beings have an innate worth and dignity because all are created by God and bear the divine image. As echoed in Proverbs 22:2, "The rich and the poor have this in common: the Lord is the maker of them all."

So far we have been speaking of the fundamental basis of human worth and dignity as grounded in creation. But Scripture also tells us that our worth is grounded in redemption, or as more commonly expressed in Christian theology, in atonement. Theologically speaking, atonement is a term referring to the saving work of Jesus Christ on the cross.

The Bible has no single explanation of how atonement "worked." Particular biblical passages can be cited as support for each of several theories of the atonement. The important point for our purposes is not in the details of the theories but in two broad claims that underlie them. First, all the theories of atonement share the conviction that somehow or other the cross of Jesus Christ has restored or made possible the restoration of a right relationship between human beings and God, and, second, that work of restoration or reconciliation has been for the benefit of each and every person. Christ died for all, for the whole world.

The saving work of Jesus Christ is not reserved for any single social class of people, rich or poor or in between. As to the extent of the atonement, "God shows no partiality" (Acts 10:34). Each person regardless of class, race, or gender is saved by unmerited grace. The saving work of Christ confirms the worth and dignity of each and every person.

You Always Have the Poor

Perhaps the best-known biblical passage about the poor is one frequently taken completely out of context. In three of the Gospels (Matthew 26:11; Mark 14:7; John 12:8) a verse appears on the lips of Jesus: "you always have the poor with you." This utterance is often taken as an excuse for ignoring poor people. After all, so this line of thinking goes, there is always going to be poverty; it's inevitable. But this interpretation is just the opposite of what the verse means in its Gospel context and its original context.

In the Gospel context, a woman anoints Jesus with a costly ointment. Some of those who witness her action object that the money would have been better spent alleviating the needs of the poor. Jesus replies by commending the woman's extravagant devotion. She has given silent testimony to Jesus' identity as the Messiah (which means "anointed one") and has symbolically prepared for his burial, anticipating his suffering and death for others. So in the context of these three Gospels, the point of the story is to call us to extravagant devotion to Jesus.[2]

When Jesus says, "You always have the poor with you," he is alluding to Deuteronomy 15:11: "there will never cease to be some in need on the earth." This statement, however, is preceded by an appeal for economic sharing and followed by the directive to "open your hand to the poor and needy neighbor." We will look more closely at the laws about the Sabbatical Year in the following section. For now, it is sufficient to note that far from justifying casual disregard for the poor, Jesus is presupposing that his listeners will respond to poverty within the framework of the covenant community.[3]

The Torah

The Pentateuch (the first five books of the Old Testament, the written Torah) testifies throughout to God's fierce and persistent concern for those who are oppressed. Early in the book of Exodus we read of God's concern when all of the Israelites are oppressed as slaves in Egypt (Exodus 2:23–25). Immediately after getting Moses's attention with a burning bush that did not burn up, God again declares his compassion for the people of Israel:

> Then the Lord said, "I have observed the misery of my people who are in Egypt; I have heard their cry on account of their taskmasters. Indeed, I know their sufferings, and I have come down to deliver them from the Egyptians, and to bring them up out of that land to a good and broad land, a land flowing with milk and honey. (Exodus 3:7–8)

Note that God not only sees, hears, and knows the suffering of the people, but God comes down into the midst of trouble and need. God, working in part through Moses, leads the people out of slavery into freedom.

Deuteronomy 26:5–9 reports a confessional recital to be made on the occasion of the offering of first fruits to God after the late summer harvest. The confession and the occasion for its use link salvation history and the agricultural cycle, the liberating God of the exodus and the Creator. This confession makes three important claims.[4] First, it describes the poverty of the Israelites in Egypt not as a "natural" or inevitable condition but as a direct result of decisions made by the Egyptians for political and economic reasons. Second, God does not tolerate the oppression of the poor and vulnerable. Poverty and oppression are counter to God's intention. Third, God provides the Israelites with a fertile land so they can support themselves and not fall back into slavery. The gift to the land is essential to breaking the cycle of poverty. These three assertions characterize the core of what the Bible has to say about poverty and the poor.

When Israel as a whole is oppressed, the Lord leads them out of slavery. When Israel inherits the land, God emerges as the protector of those groups and individuals who are landless.

> You shall not wrong or oppress a resident alien, for you were aliens in the land of Egypt. You shall not abuse any widow or orphan. If you do abuse them, when they cry out to me, I will surely heed their cry. (Exodus 22:21–23; see also Deuteronomy 10:17–19)

With the loss of a primary breadwinner and with no inheritance rights, the situation of widows and orphans in ancient Israel was precarious. Resident aliens, barred from owning land, were likewise vulnerable to economic disaster and to mistreatment. The obligation to care for widows, orphans, and sojourners rests on the mercies of God already bestowed on all God's people.

The legal traditions in the Torah stipulate certain rights of the poor and corresponding duties of more successful members of the community. For instance, employees are prohibited from withholding the wages of day laborers (Leviticus 19:13; Deuteronomy 24:14–15). The legal provision for gleaning required that landowners not be excessively efficient in harvesting crops (Leviticus 19:9–10; 23:22; Deuteronomy 24:19–22). Gleaning provided a double benefit for poor members of the community. Along with the food gathered, gleaning—because it required work—provided the poor with a degree of dignity. The triennial tithe was one means of providing assistance to poor people (as well as Levites, who owned no land) on a regular basis (Deuteronomy 14:28–29). Perhaps even more significant was the practice of extending interest-free loans (Exodus 22:25; Leviticus 25:35–38; Deuteronomy 23:19–20).[5] When a loan to a poor person involves collateral, the Torah is explicit in protecting both the physical well-being and the dignity of the one borrowing (Exodus 22:26; Deuteronomy 24:10–13).

The rights and duties cited are generally ameliorative efforts in response to the needs of those living on the edge of economic disaster. But the legal traditions in the Pentateuch go even further. In a society in which poverty and slavery were not part of God's intention and not supposed to exist, some provisions are needed to help those who have already suffered economic disaster to recover. For any number of reasons—death and disability of the breadwinner, drought, poor judgment, exploitation by those with wealth and power—peasant farmers with barely enough resources to provide for themselves and their families could slip into poverty and not be able to escape. A similar risk of ruin and destitution would have accompanied loans for commercial purposes that were common at a later stage of Israel's history. Debts accumulate and become crushing burdens. When economic hardships compounded, sometimes the only way for a poor person to survive was to become a slave. But if God's intention is that all persons in a community should flourish, some means of breaking the cycle of poverty that keeps the poor in economic dependency is needed. The Torah provides for three such radical measures.

Forgiveness of Debts

One of those radical measures is the stipulation that debts are to be forgiven every seven years. Deuteronomy 15:1–11 describes this feature of the sabbatical year and is worth quoting in its entirety.

> Every seventh year you shall grant a remission of debts. And this is the manner of the remission: every creditor shall remit the claim that is held against a neighbor, not exacting it of a neighbor who is a member of the community, because the Lord's remission has been proclaimed. Of a foreigner you may exact it, but you must remit your claim on whatever any member of your community owes you. There will, however, be no one in need among you, because the Lord is sure to bless you in the land that the Lord your God is giving you as a possession to occupy, if only you will obey the Lord your God by diligently observing this entire commandment that I command you today. When the Lord your God has blessed you, as he promised you, you will lend to many nations, but you will not borrow; you will rule over many nations, but they will not rule over you. If there is among you anyone in need, a member of your community in any of your towns within the land that the Lord your God is giving you, do not be hard-hearted or tight-fisted toward your needy neighbor. You should rather open your hand, willingly lending enough to meet the need, whatever it may be. Be careful that you do not entertain a mean thought, thinking, "The seventh year, the year of remission, is near," and therefore view your needy neighbor with hostility and give nothing; your neighbor might cry to the Lord against you, and you would incur guilt. Give liberally and be ungrudging when you do so, for on this account the Lord your God will bless you in all your work and in all that you undertake. Since there will never cease to be some in need on the earth, I therefore command you, "Open your hand to the poor and needy neighbor in your land." (Deuteronomy 15:1–11)

In a land full of God's blessing and where the people obey the Lord's instruction, there should not be any people who are poor (verse 4). This is God's intention, the way life is supposed to be. But the Bible is realistic. Inevitably, in a sinful and broken world, some people will fall into poverty (verse 11). To help close the gap between the divine intention that everyone in the community should flourish economically and the recognition that some people do not, compassionate sharing is needed, expected, and even required.

Poor people are not to be considered outcasts of the society; rather, they are to be regarded and accepted as neighbors. Notice how often the passage refers to those in debt as a member of the community, a neighbor (verses 2, 3, 7, 9, 11). The assumption is that all Israelites, whether rich or poor, belong to one family under God. One's sisters and brothers have a legitimate claim on one's compassion and care.

Every seventh year, debts are to be cancelled so that everyone gets a fresh start, breaking the cycle of poverty. The motivation for this bold action comes from an attitude of generosity. Do not be heard-hearted (verse 7) and do not entertain a mean or hostile thought toward your neighbor (verse 9). Do not rationalize ignoring poor persons in the community. As biblical scholar Patrick Miller summarizes, "compassion and openheartedness are the order of God, attitudes that work themselves out in the action of the hand, which, like the heart, must be open and not closed."[6]

Release from Debt-Slavery

A second radical measure that marries conscience and legislative action to counter poverty in ancient Israel had to do with debt-slavery (see Exodus 21:2; Leviticus 25:39–41; Deuteronomy 15:12–14). Exodus 21:2, which is part of the covenant code, a collection of laws generally regarded by scholars as the oldest of the Pentateuchal law codes, specifies release of slaves after six years. Deuteronomy 15:12–14, which is part of a later strand of tradition, does the same, but adds the requirement to provide one's newly freed slave with the material wherewithal to navigate successfully the transition to self-sufficiency. Leviticus 25:39–41, which is part of the description of the year of jubilee, stipulates that slaves are to be released every fiftieth year.

The assumption in all three passages is that while circumstances may force people into slavery, debt-slavery is not supposed to be a permanent condition. The purpose underlying all three passages is to break the cycle of poverty and dependency, to restore human freedom and dignity to the poor.

Returning Land to Its Original Owner

The third radical measure in the Torah intended to prevent an ever-widening gap between the landed and the landless, the rich and the poor, was also part of the year of jubilee (Leviticus 25:10, 13, 23). The return of land to its ancestral owners every half century was meant to keep the rich from growing richer across generations and the poor from growing poorer across generations. Whether or not the jubilee year was ever actually observed, its inclusion in the Bible suggests a recognition that vast disparities between rich and poor are not conducive to the healthy community that God desires.

All three of these radical measures—forgiveness of debts, release from debt-slavery, and restoration of land to its original owners—point to an underlying principle.[7] There must be regular ways of allowing the poor to shed their burdens and chains, to recoup, to recover, to begin anew. God says *no* to any economic system that locks people into permanent debt or bondage. God says *no* to any economic system that permanently places land, or any basis for productive activity, in the hands of a few while others are denied access to the means of sustenance. God says *no* to the assumption that economic patterns and practices that result in poverty for some people are fate or destiny. Instead, God says *yes* to equity and opportunity for all members of the community, especially for those who do not have it.

The Psalms

The Psalms have been described as "humanity's words to God and as God's words to humanity."[8] God as the champion of the poor is a frequent topic in that exchange.

- "Because the poor are despoiled, because the needy groan, I will now rise up," says the Lord; "I will place them in the safety for which they long." (Psalm 12:5)
- All my bones shall say, "O Lord, who is like you? You deliver the weak from those too strong for them, the weak and needy from those who despoil them." (Psalm 35:10)
- Father of orphans and protector of widows is God in his holy habitation. (Psalm 68:5)
- For the Lord hears the needy, and does not despise his own that are in bonds. (Psalm 69:33)
- He raises the poor from the dust, and lifts the needy from the ash heap. (Psalm 113:7)
- I know that the Lord maintains the cause of the needy, and executes justice for the poor. (Psalm 140:12)
- Who executes justice for the oppressed; who gives food to the hungry. The Lord sets the prisoners free; the Lord opens the eyes of the blind. The Lord lifts up those who are bowed down; the Lord loves the righteous. The Lord watches over the strangers; he upholds the orphan and the widow, but the way of the wicked he brings to ruin. (Psalm 146:7–9)

How in practice does God establish justice for the poor and marginalized? Normally God works through earthly agents, and the psalmists saw the king as the most important earthly agent of God's heavenly rule. The king's primary responsibility is to establish the justice and righteousness that God desires. As Psalm 72:1–4, 7, 12–14 makes clear, the standard for evaluating the king's administration of justice and righteousness is how the poor, the weak, the most vulnerable are treated.

Eighth Century Prophets

By the eighth century BC, social and economic power in Palestine had shifted from small landowners and farmers to the wealthy and those with political power. A two-tier social structure emerged: the rich and the poor, the powerful and the powerless. And the gains of those on top came at the expense of those on the bottom. That was a situation the prophets—especially Isaiah, Amos, Micah—found intolerable.

Biblical scholar John Donahue provides a helpful, succinct characterization of the prophetic role: "The prophet in Israel is not one who foretells, but one who *forthtells*. He speaks not with foresight into the future but with insight into the ways in which people have broken the covenant."[9] The prophet speaks both on behalf of God and on behalf of those with no voice. As Abraham Heschel puts it, "Prophecy is the voice that God has lent to the silent agony, a voice to the plundered poor, to the profaned riches of the world . . . God is raging in the prophets' words."[10] The prophets proclaim that faithfulness to the God of the covenant must be demonstrated in concern for the poor and oppressed.

Chapters 1–39 of the book of Isaiah are generally associated with Isaiah ben Amoz, who prophesized in the southern kingdom of Judah in the eighth century BC. It was a time of increasing urbanization and a growing divide between those comfortably well off and those struggling for survival.

Isaiah castigates those prosperous and greedy members of society who find ways to confiscate the houses and fields of their vulnerable neighbors:

> Ah, [woe to] you who join house to house, who add field to field, until there is room for no one but you, and you are left to live alone in the midst of the land! (Isaiah 5:8)

Such amassing of huge estates is a grave violation of God's intent as revealed in the Torah.

In numerous passages, Isaiah denounces the powerful for their treatment of the poor:

- The Lord enters into judgment with the elders and princes of his people: It is you who have devoured the vineyard; the spoil of the poor is in your houses. What do you mean by crushing my people, by grinding the face of the poor? says the Lord God of hosts. (Isaiah 3:14–15)
- Your princes are rebels and companions of thieves. Everyone loves a bribe and runs after gifts. They do not defend the orphan, and the widow's cause does not come before them. (Isaiah 1:23)
- Ah, you who make iniquitous decrees, who write oppressive statutes, to turn aside the needy from justice and to rob the poor of my people of their right, that widows may be your spoil, and that you may make the orphans your prey! (Isaiah 10:1–2)

Notice that treatment of the especially vulnerable—widows and orphans—is a litmus test of justice in the community.

Isaiah holds fast to a glimmer of hope that Judah can be reconciled with God. But this can happen only if profound changes are made:

> Wash yourselves; make yourselves clean; remove the evil of your doings from before my eyes; cease to do evil, learn to do good; seek justice, rescue the oppressed, defend the orphan, plead for the widow. (Isaiah 1:16–17)

The prophet Micah grew up in a small town in the foothills of Judah and directed his speeches primarily at the residents of Jerusalem. Micah shows less interest in the covenant with David and Jerusalem and much more interest in the covenant with Moses and Israel. The reason Jerusalem will fall is precisely because Judah is not obeying the terms of the Mosaic covenant, which requires Israel to maintain justice for the poor and vulnerable after itself having experienced injustice in Egypt.

Micah 2:1–2 in particular resonates with Isaiah 5:8:

> Alas for those who devise wickedness and evil deeds on their beds! When the morning dawns, they perform it, because it is in their power. They covet fields, and seize them; houses, and take them away; they oppress householder and house, people and their inheritance. (Micah 2:1–2)

Covetousness is the root of the problem here, in violation of the Tenth Commandment. The powerful have found ways to circumvent the laws protecting the holdings of small farmers. Such avarice violates the ideal of ancient Israel as a nation of free landholders. The land is God's gift. Seizing the property of the poor violates the covenant and robs the people of their identity and independence.

One of the most beloved passages of Scripture comes from Micah, insisting that true religion is more a matter of how we live on a day-to-day basis than a matter of religious practices:

> "With what shall I come before the Lord, and bow myself before God on high? Shall I come before him with burnt offerings, with calves a year old? Will the Lord be pleased with thousands of rams, with ten thousands of rivers of oil? Shall I give my firstborn for my transgression, the fruit of my body for the sin of my soul?" He has told you, O mortal, what is good; and what does the Lord

require of you but to do justice, and to love kindness, and to walk humbly with your God? (Micah 6:6–8)

Doing justice is more than wishing for it. Doing justice is working for equity—fairness in the courts and in the distribution of goods—for all, especially the powerless. Doing justice entails being an advocate for those who are hurting and in need.

The prophet Amos was originally from a town in Judah, but the setting for his prophecy is the northern kingdom of Israel. During the rule of King Jeroboam II, Israel was temporarily free from outside military threats and enjoying remarkable prosperity. But Amos recognizes that something is rotten at the core of that society. He is adamant that the behavior of the ruling class violates the principles of social justice embedded in the Torah (Amos 2:6–8). The powerful sell poor people into slavery for trifling debts (the price of sandals) and take bribes to convict the poor in courts (the city gate). Female slaves are sexually exploited. The wealthy misuse clothes taken as loan collateral and the powerful misappropriate public fines for their own self-indulgenced. Wealthy landowners take more than a fair share of the crop as rent for the land (Amos 5:11a)

Amos denounces superficial religiosity in the three great festivals and in other worship gatherings and attacks the sacrificial system. The posture and trappings of religious ceremony mean nothing without justice:

> I hate, I despise your festivals, and I take no delight in your solemn assemblies. Even though you offer me your burnt offerings and grain offerings, I will not accept them; and the offerings of well-being of your fatted animals I will not look upon. Take away from me the noise of your songs; I will not listen to the melody of your harps. But let justice roll down like waters, and righteousness like an everflowing stream. (Amos 5:21–24)

Jesus and the Gospels

The kingdom of God is the central image in the preaching and teaching of Jesus. The kingdom (the active reign or rule of God) is a present reality that requires a response (Mark 1:15; Matthew 4:17, 4:23, 9:35; Luke 10:9, 11:20, 17:21), and the kingdom has yet to come in its fullness (Matthew 6:10).

As a symbol, the kingdom carries the overtones of meanings it has in the Old Testament.[11] This is perhaps nowhere more clear than in Jesus' programmatic declaration of the nature of his ministry in Luke 4:16–21. In the two passages that Jesus draws on, Isaiah 58:6 and 61:1–2 and in the allusion to the year of jubilee in Leviticus 25, the concept of *release* and *liberty* loom large. Jesus announces that the intention and goal of his ministry is to carry out the purpose of God set forth in the Torah and the prophets. Some passages throughout the New Testament certainly proclaim release of a different sort: release from sin and guilt—that is, forgiveness. But Jesus' explicit connection here to the Old Testament witness about *release* clearly suggests that what God is doing in Jesus is not merely release from sin and guilt but also release from all kinds of physical, social, and economic oppression.

The Gospel of Luke shows a special concern for the poor.[12] We will look at only one other Lucan passage that deals specifically with the poor: the parable of the rich man and Lazarus (Luke 16:19–31). This story, following close on the heels of Jesus' warning that it is not possible to serve both God and wealth (Luke 16:13) is addressed to those "who were lovers of money" (Luke 16:14). Several things about the parable warrant comment. First, nothing is said about the merit of Lazarus; he is simply destitute. Second, while the rich man enjoys a lavish lifestyle, there is no suggestion that he came by his fortune dishonestly or that he directly exploited Lazarus. Third, the rich man simply ignored Lazarus. He is guilty only of failing to feel compassion and to extend hospitality to the poor man at his gate. Fourth, Abraham tells the rich man that the requirement to act justly and mercifully to the poor comes from the Torah and the prophets. Fifth, the parable implies that the kingdom God belongs to the poor. The rich may enter if they treat the poor with kindness.

The Gospel of Matthew includes a story equally comforting or disturbing—depending on one's perspective. Matthew 25:31–46 tells of the judgment of all the nations (the whole earth) that will take place at the Parousia (when Christ returns). Judgment turns on the treatment of the hungry, the thirsty, strangers, the naked, the sick and those in prison. The surprising twist in the story is that neither the "sheep" who are commended nor the "goats" who are condemned knew that Jesus Christ is present in "the least of these" poor and needy people.[13]

The Early Christian Church

The sociopolitical context of the early church was dramatically different than that of ancient Israel. The early church was a tiny minority scattered across the huge Roman Empire. But within the community of believers an ideal of mutual care emerged (see Acts 2:44–45, 4:32, 4:34–35). We have reason to suspect that the ideal was seldom fully in practice. But to the degree that it was achieved, poverty was alleviated or eliminated from early Christian communities.

Paul's letters to early Christian communities give us a less idyllic picture of what was happening in the early house churches. The church at Corinth provides one example. In 1 Corinthians 1:26 Paul writes, "Not many of you were wise by human standards, not many were powerful, not many were of noble birth." But the implication is that some of the Corinthians were educated, powerful, and wealthy. Confirmation that church members were of unequal social backgrounds is provided by Paul's strong objection to some Corinthians bringing lawsuits against fellow Christians in civil courts (1 Corinthians 6:1–11). Roman civil courts gave a huge advantage to the rich who routinely bribed judges with gifts or favors. So wealthy Christians were using their superior social power to take goods, land, and money from poor Christians. Paul would have none if it! The church is supposed to be an alternative community, not a mere reflection of status-conscious Roman culture.

The division between social classes in the church at Corinth underlies Paul's scathing criticism of abuses at the Lord's Supper (1 Corinthians 11:17–22). The community of believers would gather at the large home of a wealthy member to share the symbolic bread and cup as part of an actual meal. Following Roman social convention, the wealthy friends of the host would have places of comfort and privilege in the dining room and would consume the best of the food and drink. Poorer members of the church would be left in the courtyard, hungry and humiliated. Paul regards such practices as an outrage. The church is not supposed to mirror the division between rich and poor that is present in the surrounding culture.

In Galatians 3:28, Paul is probably quoting an early baptismal liturgical formula.

> There is no longer Jew or Greek, there is no longer slave or free, there is no longer male and female; for all of you are one in Christ Jesus. (Galatians 3:28)

In early practice, candidates for baptism would take off their own clothes—and whatever status symbols the clothes carried—and be baptized naked, then dress in plain identical white robes, symbolizing purity and community and new life. The stark symbolism of the baptismal act and the radical nature of the liturgical formula reflect the new creation that God has brought into being.

The church is an alternative community in which old social inequalities are being overturned and transformed. Ethnic distinctions no longer matter. Distinctions of social class and power are negated. Gender distinctions have lost their power to divide and oppress. The basis of this unity in the church is Christ.

While Paul believed that Christ's return was imminent, this belief did not lead him to ignore the needs of the poor. During his travels, he took up a collection for the poor of the church in Jerusalem (Romans 15:25–27; 1 Corinthians 16:1–4; 2 Corinthians 8–9; Galatians 2:1–10). To Paul's way of thinking, there should be a "fair balance" between those who have an abundance and those whose needs are great. Christians who have financial resources are to help those Christians who are poor.

Finally, let's look briefly at the Letter of James. The letter is not addressed to a specific church; rather, it is a general letter to be circulated among several churches. Three passages are especially relevant for our purpose. James 1:27 provides a succinct description of authentic faith. James's concern for the poor, orphans, and widows in particular harkens back to the Torah. James 2:1–9 tackles the problem of discrimination against the poor within the church. As we have seen, God's concern for the poor is familiar biblical teaching from the Torah, Psalms, and the prophets. The commandment to love your neighbor as yourself is drawn from Leviticus 19:18. The adjective *royal* suggests that the love command is the law of the kingdom of God.

James is perfectly clear that Christians should attend to the material needs of poor brothers and sisters in the faith:

> What good is it, my brothers and sisters, if you say you have faith but do not have works? Can faith save you? If a brother or sister is naked and lacks daily food, and one of you says to them, "Go in peace; keep warm and eat your fill," and yet you do not supply their bodily needs, what is the good of that? So faith by itself, if it has no works, is dead. (James 2:14–17)

Since the time of Martin Luther, some have mistakenly seen a sharp disagreement between James and Paul about faith and works. Paul and James are using "works" in two very different ways. Paul refers to work of the law, meaning commandments such as circumcision or dietary rules. When James speaks of works he means deeds of mercy that are expected of Christians. Paul would have agreed with James that faith that doesn't produce appropriate deeds is not genuine faith.

Conclusion

The Bible bears witness throughout to God's passion for justice in human communities and to God's special concern for those who are poor, vulnerable, marginalized, or oppressed. The Bible consistently declares that God is sovereign over all of history and creation. The biblical writers observe that God normally exercises this sovereignty incarnationally—that is, through human agents. Human beings are charged with carrying out in practice God's concern for the well-being of the poor, making it manifest in compassionate generosity and, even more important, in justice.

In the early period of Israel's life, when it was a tribal confederacy, the Torah places responsibility for the well-being of the poor on the whole community. During the period of the monarchy (in both the united kingdom and the later divided kingdoms), the authority and obligation to vouchsafe the rights of the poor was vested in the king. The fledgling Christian church remembered the teachings of Jesus that love of neighbor knows no ethnic or geographic boundaries (see Luke 10:25–37) but gave particular attention to the responsibility of Christians to be a peculiar community that embraced and honored the poor as full members. So what do we do? Our social world is neither a theocratic tribal confederacy nor a monarchy. Many of us are citizens in a global empire, but it is not Rome. God still chooses to be at work through human agents, within and beyond the church. God uses us as instruments to demonstrate mercy and to establish justice for the poor. Scripture does not dictate that Christians adopt any particular economic system. But the Bible does suggest some constants across the centuries. Threats to the social fabric of society are not a new phenomenon. The God who spoke long ago as the defender of the poor and oppressed is the same Lord we worship as supremely revealed in Jesus Christ. The call for mercy and justice that pervades the Bible is directed to all of us who claim the Old and New Testaments as Scripture.

The strategies by which the poor are protected and lifted up are particular to each era and situation. But the purposes and principles that prompt those biblical strategies abide. Concern for poor people should find expression in acts of mercy and justice; faithfulness to God requires no less. The church is called to be an alternative society, characterized by solidarity with the poor. And the community of faith is called to take action as a body and as individual members on behalf of the poor. We do so not only out of obligation but because it is who we are as the people of God.

Notes

1. The second account of creation (Genesis 2:4–25) draws from a different strand of tradition to make a congruent point. The human being is placed in the Garden of Eden to "till it and keep it" (Genesis 2:15), to cultivate it and protect it.

2. Richard B. Hays, "You Always Have the Poor with You," *Biblical Literacy Today* 3, no. 2 (Winter 1988–1989), 3.

3. Ibid.

4. Leslie J. Hoppe, *There Shall Be No Poor Among You: Poverty in the Bible* (Nashville: Abingdon Press, 2004), 18.

5. See John Mason, "Assisting the Poor: Assistance Programmes in the Bible," *Transformation* (April–June 1987): 1–14, cited in Stephen Mott and Ronald J. Sider, "Economic Justice: A Biblical Paradigm" in *Toward a Just and Caring Society: Christian Responses to Poverty in America*, ed. David P. Gushee (Grand Rapids: Baker Books, 1999), 15–45, 521–535.

6. Patrick D. Miller, *Deuteronomy. Interpretation: A Bible Commentary for Teaching and Preaching* (Louisville: John Knox, 1990), 136.

7. Ibid., 138–139.

8. J. Clinton McCann, "The Book of Psalms: Introduction, Commentary, and Reflections," in *The New Interpreter's Bible*, vol. 4, ed. Leander E. Keck (Nashville: Abingdon Press, 1996), 642.

9. John R. Donahue, "Biblical Perspectives on Justice," in *The Faith That Does Justice*, ed. John C. Haughey (New York: Paulist Press, 1977), 74.

10. Abraham J. Heschel, *The Prophets* (New York: Harper & Row, 1962), 5.

11. Donahue, "Biblical Perspectives on Justice," 86.

12. See the discussion in Hoppe, *There Shall Be No Poor Among You*, 150–155.

13. See the fuller discussion of "the least of these" in Thomas G. Long, *Matthew: Westminster Bible Companion* (Louisville: Westminster John Knox, 1997), 283–286.

Tiwarin Duangkam participates in a dance group organized by the Hualin Buddhist Temple in the northern Thailand village of Toong-sa-tok. Ms. Duangkam, 13 and HIV negative, lost her mother to AIDS and lives with her HIV positive father. *(Paul Jeffrey)*

Chapter 3

Our United Methodist Heritage

Kenneth L. Carder

Toward the end of his long and productive life, John Wesley reflected on the movement he had led for five decades. On the surface, signs of success abounded. The number of Methodists in the British Isles had grown from a small group of students at Oxford to approximately seventy thousand, with another eighty thousand in America. Institutions for learning, health care, and publishing had been established, and the newly formed church in America was expanding rapidly in numbers and influence.

Wesley's assessment of the success of "the people called Methodists," however, was ambivalent at best. He wondered if perhaps he had "sown wild grapes" and feared that the movement was in danger of losing its spiritual and evangelical power. In the opening paragraph of "Thoughts upon Methodism," written in 1786, Wesley mused:

> I am not afraid that the people called Methodists should ever cease to exist in either Europe or America. But I am afraid lest they should only exist as a dead sect, having the form of religion without the power. And this undoubtedly will be the case unless they hold fast both the doctrine, spirit, and discipline with which they first set out.[1]

The major threat identified by Wesley in this brief recounting of the development of Methodism and in several sermons was the growing prosperity of the Methodists. They were becoming wealthy! Wesley considered that the increase in wealth was resulting in a decrease in reliance on grace, a lack of discipline, and separation from the poor. Material prosperity threatened that which Wesley considered constitutive to Christian discipleship—friendship with, aid to, and advocacy on behalf of the poor.

The recovery of our heritage among the poor is key to renewal of United Methodism in the twenty-first century. Whereas Methodism began as a movement among the poor who helped to shape its mission, beliefs, and practices, contemporary United Methodism is predominantly a middle-class denomination. Recovery of our heritage among the people who live in poverty, which is the majority of the world's people, may be the most promising means of assuring that United Methodism exists as more than "a dead sect, having the form of religion without the power."

John Wesley and the Poor

Samuel Wesley and Susanna Wesley knew firsthand the struggles of those with meager financial resources. Though an educated and respected priest in the Anglican Church, Samuel Wesley spent time in debtors' prison at Lincoln and struggled to meet the basic needs of a growing family. In 1708 a fire destroyed the rectory at Epworth and all of the family's possessions. Five-year-old John was the last one rescued, barely escaping the roaring flames. John and Susanna emphasized the providential deliverance of all the children. However, at some point the focus began to center on John, who by 1737 had adopted for himself the phrase from the Old Testament prophets: "a brand plucked out of the burning" (Amos 4:11; Zechariah 3:2). Such traumatic threat and loss undoubtedly contributed to John Wesley's sense of calling to and empathy for those who lived with scarcity and insecurity.

As young men at Oxford, John and Charles, along with four or five others, set out to pursue a life of holiness, which John Wesley defined as total love for God and neighbor. Among the practices to which they committed themselves were meeting together for Bible study and theological reflection, persistent prayer, and visitation of the poor and imprisoned. By 1730 they were spending several hours each week with the poor and needy. They soon expanded their concern to include persons incarcerated in the city jail and began bringing together for tutoring and support children of poor families in Oxford. Their consistent acts of piety and compassion eventually came to the attention of other students and members of the university community. They were mocked as "the Holy Club," "Bible Moths," "Godly Club," and eventually the term "Methodist" was applied to them. The name *Methodist* from the very beginning signified the pursuit of holiness through acts of devotion and compassion, especially among the poor.

John Wesley's vocational commitment reached a turning point in 1738 and 1739. Early in 1738 Wesley returned from his two years as a priest and missionary in the U.S. state of Georgia. His efforts in Georgia were modestly successful at best, and he returned to his homeland discouraged and facing a vocational and faith crisis. He thought about giving up preaching as the consequence of his lack of faith. It was the Lutheran minister Peter Bohler who admonished him: "Preach faith *till* you have it, and then, *because* you have it, you will preach faith."[2]

The journal entry for March 6, 1738, is equally pivotal, although far less noted by interpreters of Wesley: "The first person to whom I offered *salvation by faith* alone was a prisoner under the sentence of death. His name was [William] Clifford."[3] It was the witness of the power of God to transform a death row inmate convicted of assault, burglary, and desertion that confirmed the validity of Bohler's advice and offered promise to the restless Wesley that he might know this inner assurance of salvation. May 24, 1738, is a date deeply etched in the Methodist heritage, the occasion of Wesley's "heartwarming experience" while attending a society meeting at Aldersgate Street. The assurance of salvation that Wesley had witnessed in William Clifford two months earlier now became his own experience.

While Wesley's Aldersgate experience represents an important turning point, April 2, 1739, marked the beginning of the Methodist revival. At the invitation and urging of George Whitefield, Wesley preached his first sermon in the open air near Bristol. The crowd consisted predominantly of miners, laborers, and the poor. As his text, he chose the words of Jesus' inaugural sermon in Nazareth, taken from the prophetic tradition of the Old Testament: "The Spirit of the Lord is upon me, because he has anointed me to bring good news to the poor. He has sent me to proclaim release to the captives and recovery of sight to the blind, to let the oppressed go free, to proclaim the year of the Lord's favor" (Luke 4:18–19; Isaiah 61:1–2).

Henceforth, the poor and marginalized of society played a central role in shaping Methodism's mission, beliefs, practices, and structures. The records indicate that Wesley intentionally turned toward the poor as the focus of his personal relationships and ministry. To his critics in the established church, he said, "The honourable, the great, we are thoroughly willing (if it be the will of the Lord) to leave to you. Only let us alone with the poor, the vulgar, the base, the outcasts of men."[4]

Wesley loved the poor, often staying in their hovels, sharing their food, even catching their diseases and lice. Every activity of the early Methodist movement was influenced by the impact on the poor—the venue of the preaching, the composition and agenda of the classes and bands, the institutions formed, even the style of the preaching houses, which were to be plain and inexpensive. Near the end of his life, Wesley validated God's action among the Methodists with this assessment: "And surely never in any age or nation, since the Apostles, have these words been so eminently fulfilled, 'the poor have the gospel preached unto them,' as it is at this day."[5]

Personal Engagement with the Poor

Wesley's relationship with the poor included personal friendship and aid, establishing institutions designed to address systemic needs and issues, advocacy, evangelization, and stewardship development. He regarded such visitation as a crucial aspect of Christian discipleship, and he could no more imagine a week without visiting the poor than he could a week without participation in public worship and the Eucharist. He insisted that visiting the poor was an essential means of grace and a necessary expression of obedience to Christ.

Class divisions characterized eighteenth century England as they do American society today. Wesley understood that widespread apathy and prejudice toward the poor resulted from the failure by the prosperous to form relationships with the poor. He declared, "One great reason why the rich in general, have so little sympathy for the poor, is, because they so seldom visit them."[6] To guard against paternalism and stereotyping, Wesley insisted that aid be delivered directly to the poor rather than sent from a detached distance. Thus, the practice of visiting the poor broke down barriers between the classes and "*broadened* the concept of community to include everyone, from the top to the bottom of the economic scale."[7] Wesley cultivated empathy for the poor in the leaders among the Methodists, as evident in his directive to the society stewards: "If you cannot relieve, do not grieve, the poor. Give them soft words, if nothing else. . . . Put yourself in the place of every poor [person] and deal with *him* as you would God should deal with you."[8]

Visiting the poor wherever they resided, in homes or prisons, was part of Wesley's vision of a community in which everyone's needs would be sufficiently met. Such a community would provide for one another the resources necessary for flourishing as beloved children of God. Necessary resources included adequate food and clothing, shelter, education, and medical care. Wesley personally solicited money to aid the poor throughout his life. One of the most poignant entries in his journal occurs January 4, 1785, when he is eighty-two years old:

> At this season [Christmas] we usually distribute coals and bread among the poor of the society [of London]. But I now considered, they wanted clothes as well as food. So on this and the four following days, I walked through the town, and begged two hundred pounds in order to clothe them that needed it most. But

it was hard work, as most of the streets were filled with melting snow, which often lay ankle deep; so that my feet were steeped in snow-water nearly from morning till evening.[9]

His diary indicates that he spent about thirty hours in personal solicitations that week. The amount collected equals about $30,000 in today's currency. Collecting such a large amount required that Wesley approach the rich and prosperous in the classes and societies. The "begging" was made easier because the poor on behalf of whom Wesley made the solicitation were known personally by those from whom the aid was requested.

Establishing Institutions

But the aid went beyond personal friendship and almsgiving. Wesley and the Methodists established institutions that addressed systemic needs of the poor and enabled them to help themselves—schools for children of the poor, credit unions, and cooperatives for the working poor, free health clinics, and pensions for "worn out preachers."

Throughout his life, Wesley was interested in the education of children, including children of the poor. He supported existing charity schools and started schools for poor children himself, the first being located in Oxford.[10]

As another tool for the education of the poor, Wesley promoted publication of inexpensive tracts and abridgements and even whole libraries, making them accessible to those with limited resources. He even suggested that his preachers should "beg from the rich to buy books for the poor."[11]

Wesley was aware that the poor included people who were underemployed and going through hard times at no fault of their own. A lending program was established in 1748 to assist such persons. Wesley raised thirty pounds to provide seed money to help small businesses, primarily tradesmen, merchants, and manufacturers. The money was loaned at no interest for a period of three months. According to Richard Heitzenrater, 255 people were assisted with loans during the first eighteen months, and the program continued for years.[12]

Wesley had a special interest in medicine, and the health of the poor was a focus of the Methodist movement. He took pride in the origins of the clinics for the poor that he started at the Foundry, the place where he organized his ministry, in the late 1740s. The original intent was to provide care for the members of the Foundry Society, but of the more than one hundred who came the first few months, several were strangers to Wesley. The Foundry clinic is considered the first free public medical dispensary in London, and he later made similar services available at Newcastle and Bristol.[13]

A primary source of medical assistance to the poor was the collection of home remedies for common illnesses titled *Primitive Physick*. It was an expanded version of an earlier brief publication in 1745 with the title *A Collection of Receits for the Use of the Poor*, which clearly demonstrates that his primary focus was to assist the poor. Prominent among the entries are remedies for conditions common among the poor, such as "itch." The volume went through nearly two dozen editions in Wesley's lifetime. Although many of the remedies seem quaint today, *Primitive Physick* illustrates Wesley's concern that medical care be available to those who could least afford it.[14]

Advocacy on Behalf of the Poor

Wesley's commitment to the poor is also reflected in his advocacy on their behalf and his challenge of injustice and economic disparity. He was often in direct conflict with powerful sectors of eighteenth century

English society, especially the exploitive practices of the medical and legal professions. He strongly denounced business practices that took advantage of the poor, such as usury and the liquor industry. He denounced slavery and the slave trade as a heinous evil. His solidarity with the poor enabled him to evaluate policies and practices in terms of their impact on the poor.

In Thoughts on the Present Scarcity of Provisions,[15] Wesley addresses the prevalence and causes of poverty and advocates for societal changes that enable the poor to rise from their plight. Wesley vehemently challenged the notion that the number languishing in poverty was small and that their poverty resulted from their own "idleness." He attributes the poverty to unemployment resulting from unjust policies and practices. Such policies caused various commodities to become so expensive that the majority of the people could not afford them and the demand for goods had decreased, leading to unemployment. For example, he suggested that half the corn crop went to distilleries. Thus, his strong opposition to the distilling business grew out of concern for the effects of the business on the poor. Wesley also protested the emergence of large farm monopolies that put tenant farmers off the land. Produce heretofore produced by small farmers such as poultry and pork became rarer and costlier. The land was used to satisfy the appetites for luxuries of the aristocracy, who wastefully consumed so much that their neighbors lacked necessities.[16] Taxation policies that favored the rich made things even worse for the poor.

Among the changes Wesley advocates are the following: prohibit distilling, tax exported horses and the gentry's carriages, reduce the size of farms so that small farmers can exist, and turn to "repressing luxury; whether by laws, by example, or both."[17] He further called for paying off the national debt (thereby reducing taxes and the price of goods) and terminating needless expenses that benefit only the prosperous.

Lifestyle and Stewardship Shaped in Response to the Poor

Wesley's commitment to economic justice and a lifestyle formed in relationship with the poor is evident in his understanding and practice of stewardship. Randy Maddox summarizes the core points of Wesley's economic ethic in four points: (1) ultimately everything belongs to God, (2) resources are placed in our care to use as God desires, (3) God desires that we use those resources to provide necessities for ourselves and our families and others in need, and (4) spending money on luxuries for ourselves while others lack necessities is robbing God.[18] Maddox adds, "While Adam Smith held that surplus accumulation was the foundation of economic well-being, Wesley viewed it (when surrounded by those in need) as mortal sin!"[19]

Wesley's theology and personal practice of stewardship is succinctly summarized in the points of an often preached sermon, "The Use of Money," in which he instructs to gain all you can, save all you can, and give all you can.[20] While some would use Wesley's formula as an endorsement of laissez-faire capitalism, such an interpretation would be a gross misreading. The sermon and his subsequent comments clearly indicate that Wesley is calling for a lifestyle of diligence, frugality, and extravagant generosity. The first rule (gain) is a call to social responsibility in the way one gains wealth. The second rule (save) is a summons to self-denial and eschewing of luxuries and superfluous spending, living simply so that others may simply live. But the main point of the threefold rule of Wesleyan stewardship lies in the third component: give all you can. Gaining and saving enable one to give, and the primary recipient of the generosity is to be the poor. Wesley put it this way:

> Save all you can, by cutting off every expense which serves only to indulge foolish desire, to gratify either the desire of the flesh, the desire

of the eye, or the pride of life. Waste nothing . . . on sin or folly, whether for yourself or your children. And then, Give all you can, or in other words give all you have to God.[21]

Wesley practiced such stewardship in his own life and ministry. Wesley and the Methodists raised large sums of money through the various collections, publishing, and other activities. Yet Wesley lived very frugally on a limited stipend. He vowed that if he died with as much as ten pounds in his personal possession he could justly be considered to have been a thief. When he died in 1791, he was carried to his grave by six paupers who were paid one pound each, thereby depleting his personal resources. The draperies used in the service were taken down and sewn into dresses for poor women of London.[22]

Theological Grounding and Motivation

What accounts for the preferential option for the poor in Wesley and "the people called Methodists"? Response to the poor is far more than a programmatic emphasis or an act of humanitarian aid. To Wesley and the Methodists, relationships and ministry with the poor has to do with who God is, where God is, what God is doing. God has a preferential presence with and action on behalf of the poor, and solidarity with the poor is essential if we are to share in God's life and mission.

The Methodist revival was propelled by a preoccupation with "holiness of heart and life" formed by *grace*. Grace, to Wesley, is the presence and power of God to create, redeem, reconcile, heal, and transform human hearts, communities, and the entire cosmos. Grace is God in Jesus Christ making all things new! Grace is universally present and works persistently to save, reconcile, renew, mend, and transform persons, communities, and the whole creation. Grace means that the image of God is in every person and that God is forever seeking to restore and bring to fulfillment the divine image. It also means that God's mission is holistic, encompassing the entire creation.

Wesley's concept of salvation is holistic and includes healing of the body and soul as well as relationships and the cosmos. He writes, "By salvation I mean, not barely (according to the vulgar notion) deliverance from hell, or going to heaven, but a present deliverance from sin, a restoration of the soul after the divine image in righteousness and true holiness, in justice, mercy, and truth."[23]

God's reconciling and transforming grace reaches the farthest ends of the universe as Wesley affirms in his sermon "The New Creation":

> All the elements . . . will be new, indeed entirely changed as to their qualities, although not as to their nature. . . . All the earth shall then be a more beautiful paradise than Adam ever saw. . . . He that sitteth upon the throne will soon change the face of all things, and give demonstrative proof to all his creatures that his mercy is over all his works.[24]

Wesley proclaims that God's grace will end suffering, violence, war, and injustice. Even the stars will remain in their course and no longer fall from the sky. He took literally the eschatological images of a "peaceable kingdom" contained in Scripture and was convinced that we can live now in the light of God's coming future. To live toward the new creation is to grow in grace and embody holiness of heart and life. Salvation through grace is experienced in community. One cannot be Christian in isolation. Wesley declared, "The gospel of Christ knows no religion but social; no holiness but social holiness."[25] He further professed, "Christianity is essentially a social religion, and that to turn it into a solitary religion is indeed to destroy it."[26] The early class meetings, bands, and societies were born from

An indigenous girl gets a drink in Pusthan, Nahuizalco, El Salvador, where community leaders have fought to protect their water resources. *(Paul Jeffrey)*

the conviction that experience of and growth in grace requires communities of support and accountability.

For Wesley, the presence of the poor in those communities of support and accountability is essential not only for the benefit of the poor but for the salvation of the prosperous. Wesley declared: "Religion must not go from the greatest to the least, or the power would appear to be of men."[27] Religion must begin where God begins, among the poor, the captives, the marginalized. The poor were not merely the objects of evangelization by the Methodists; they were also means of evangelizing the prosperous!

United Methodist doctrinal standards reflect the directives for those who "desire to flee from the wrath to come" so "that they may help each other to work out their salvation."[28] The members of the societies and classes were expected to "evidence their desire of salvation" by doing no harm and avoiding evil, by doing good and expressing mercy, and by observing the ordinances of God. Among the harm and evil to be avoided are buying and selling "spirituous liquors," excessive advertising, buying and selling goods that have not paid the duty, giving or taking things in usury (unlawful interest), wealthy display of self-indulgence, and borrowing without intending to repay.[29] *Doing good* means to be kind and merciful and seeking the well-being of all persons and "by giving food to the hungry, by clothing the naked, by visiting or helping them that are sick or in prison."[30]

Methodist doctrine clearly includes both acts of piety (the ordinances of God—Scripture reading, prayer, worship, fasting, Eucharist) and works of mercy.

Relationships with and aid to the poor was an indispensable act of mercy expected of all Methodists. Acts of mercy, therefore, were not mere acts of charity but were fundamentally means of sharing in the presence and power of God. Friendship with and aid to the poor and working for justice and equity were means of participating in God's salvation of persons, communities, nations, and the whole creation.

Wesley's relationship with and preferential option for the poor is grounded in obedience to Jesus Christ or commitment to imitating Christ. Historian Ted A. Campbell summarizes the motive for John and Charles Wesley's radical commitment to the poor in lines from a poem by Charles:

> Saviour, how few there are
> Who thy condition share,
> Few who cordially embrace,
> Love, and prize they poverty,
> Want on earth a resting-place,
> Needy and resign'd like Thee![31]

According to Campbell, the point in Charles Wesley's poem is not primarily that we ought to love and help the poor, nor that the poor have something to offer us. The primary point is the role of Christ "who, though he was in the form of God, did not regard equality with God as something to be exploited, but emptied himself, taking the form of a slave" (Philippians 2:6–7). Christians are called to be formed in the image of Jesus Christ, who was born among the poor, lived and taught and ministered among the poor, died alongside poor criminals, was buried in a barrowed tomb, and so closely identifies with the poor that what is done to them is done to him (Matthew 25:31–46).

The fundamental motive behind the Wesleys' commitment to the poor was obedience to and faith in Jesus Christ. Heitzenrater writes:

> The simple answer . . . to the question, Why did Wesley work with the poor? is, first and foremost, because Jesus did so, but also because Jesus told him to do so and would help him to do so. Renewal in the image of God entails being drawn into God's likeness, as seen in Christ—having the mind of Christ and walking as he walked.[32]

Recovering and Reappropriating Methodist Heritage Among the Poor

Methodism evolved from a renewal movement within the Church of England to a new church in America and now exists as multiple denominations on every continent. The Methodist family and those churches who trace their origins to the Wesleyan movement now consists of more than seventy million people who represent the ethnic, racial, national, and cultural diversity of the human family.[33] The various denominations within Methodism have their own unique histories and reflect their particular contexts; however, they share a common heritage in the Wesleyan revival in eighteenth century England, a theological foundation in holistic salvation, a connectional polity, and an involvement in mission. The role of the poor varies from context to context. Where the poor are integral to the church's life and mission the church is growing, specifically in Africa, Asia, and Latin America.

In America, the forerunners of The United Methodist Church (the Methodist Episcopal Church, the Methodist Episcopal Church South, the Protestant Methodist Church, and Evangelical United Brethren Church) maintained a strong commitment to the poor in the late eighteenth century and first part of the nineteenth century. Many of the Methodists in the new world were the working poor, farmers and laborers, even slaves. Some had left England to escape debts and to carve out a new life on the American frontier.

As had happened with the English Methodists in Wesley's time, the Methodists in America began to prosper. By the middle of the nineteenth century, leaders such as Bishop Matthew Simpson and others intentionally sought to enable Methodism to appeal to the more prosperous and influential people.[34] The Methodists became increasingly wealthy and politically powerful. The churches began to move from the back streets to main streets, and "plain meeting houses" gave way to more ornate facilities. The church became predominately middle class in its membership and practices.

The poor remained important to the American Methodists, but personal relationships with poor people became less prevalent. Concern for the poor was expressed largely through mission programs, financial contributions, and support of institutions such as orphanages, schools, and hospitals. Missionaries were sent to the poor within the United States and in other countries. The poor gradually and inadvertently became objects of charity rather than friends, means of grace, and integral members of the local church community. A disconnect emerged between the personal and social dimensions of discipleship and between acts of piety and acts of mercy, love for God, and love for neighbor.

Ministry to and with the poor became the specialized responsibility of select groups, institutions, and agencies. Women were the most diligent in living the Methodist heritage among the poor. The deaconess movement arose partly in response to the church's need to be among the poor, and deaconesses faithfully appropriated the Wesleyan tradition of "visiting the sick." Unsalaried and living communally, deaconesses uniformly wore simple long black dresses and a bonnet with white ties at the neck. Their simple standard attire made for economy, instant recognition, and protection as they worked in dangerous urban neighborhoods and gave them greater accessibility to and solidarity with people who lived in poverty.

Denominational agencies such as United Methodist Women, the General Board of Global Ministries, and the General Board of Church and Society and their predecessors bore the weight of addressing poverty and advocating on behalf of justice. Church-related health and welfare institutions as well as colleges and universities became less directly connected to the church and more directly connected to a broad middle-class constituency. Support for ministries among the poor at home and abroad moved from personal contact to the "Apportionments" assessed to congregations as "World Service and Conference Benevolences."

Within the past two decades United Methodists have seen a renewed interest in recovering our presence and ministry *with* the poor. Wesley scholars have brought to the forefront the prominent role the poor played in early Methodism.[35] The Council of Bishops adopted "Children and Poverty" as an Episcopal Initiative in 1995 and continued the initiative until 2004. The initiative declared that "the crisis among children and the impoverished and our theological and historical mandates demand more than additional programs and emphases. Nothing less than the reshaping of the United Methodist Church in response to the God who is among 'the least of these' is required."[36]

The elimination of poverty and ministry with the poor is currently one of the four focuses of The United Methodist Church in fulfilling the mission "to make disciples of Jesus Christ for the transformation of the world." The Council of Bishops, the General Board of Global Ministries, the General Board of Church and Society, and the Women's Division are leading efforts to reshape the church "in response to the God who is among 'the least of these.'" Thousands of local congregations are forming relationships with people who live in poverty in their own neighborhoods as well as those in other lands through Volunteers in Mission.

Mission is being redefined in our modern interconnected world.[37] We are moving beyond paternalistic charity toward partnerships and networking in which personal relationships and friendships are foundational. United Methodists in the United States are networking with people in Mozambique, Republic of Congo, and Philippines, and missionaries from the so-called "developing world" are being welcomed in more economically prosperous communities.

A statement approved by the Interagency Task Force on Ministry with the Poor identifies important guiding principles and foundations that accurately reflect our Methodist heritage.[38] Underlying the guiding principles is this foundational affirmation: relationships *with* the poor are integral to the Christian gospel and our Wesleyan heritage. Ministry *with* the poor involves loving service, addressing root causes of poverty, advocating just policies and practices, and establishing institutions that embody justice and hospitality for all God's people.

Conclusion

John Wesley's fear that "the people called Methodists" would exist only "as a dead sect, having the form of religion without the power" continues to haunt many of his heirs in the twenty-first century. Contemporary United Methodists long for renewal and a recovery of the evangelical zeal and mission fervor that characterized the movement in its beginning. Such renewal is evident in parts of the world where the church is among the poor, such as in Africa, Asia, and Latin America. We have in our Wesleyan heritage the necessary theological understanding and motivation, the practices of piety and mercy and justice, and the structures and polity that are foundational for renewal.

Heitzenrater, one of the preeminent Wesley scholars of our time, summarizes our heritage and current challenge as heirs of Wesley:

> [Wesley's] basic goal . . . was for the Methodists to imitate the life of Christ, not improve the national economy. He conceived of the problem theologically in terms of love of God and neighbor rather than in terms of defining minimum wage, improving the country's wealth, or solving a social problem. Everyone in every level of society was a child of God and deserved to be treated as such.[39] The question that faces us today is whether we . . . like Wesley, can imitate the life of Christ and conscientiously become one with the reality of poverty in order to let the deprivations of all our neighbors help shape our moral imagination, our ethical consciousness, our theological categories, and our social programs.[40]

Notes

1. From "Thoughts upon Methodism," in *The Works of John Wesley*, vol. 9: *The Methodist Societies: History, Nature, and Design*, ed. Rupert E. Davies (Nashville: Abingdon Press, 1989), 527. See also the following sermons by John Wesley: "The Causes of the Inefficacy of Christianity," "On God's Vineyard," and "The Use of Money."

2. W. Reginald Ward and Richard P. Heitzenrater, eds., *The Works of John Wesley*, vol. 18: *Journals and Diaries I* (Nashville: Abingdon Press, 1988), 228.

3. Ibid, 228.

4. "The Appeals to Men of Reason and Religion," in *The Works of John Wesley*, vol. 11, ed. Gerald R. Cragg (Nashville: Abingdon Press, 1989), 316.

5. "The Signs of the Times," in *The Works of John Wesley*, vol. 2: *Sermons II*, ed. Albert C. Outler (Nashville: Abingdon Press, 1985), 527.

6. "On Visiting the Sick," in *The Works of John Wesley*, vol. 3: *Sermons III*, ed. Albert C. Outler (Nashville: Abingdon Press, 1986), 387.

7. Richard P. Heitzenrater, "The Poor and the People Called Methodists," in *The Poor and the People Called Methodists 1729–1999*, ed. Richard P. Heitzenrater (Nashville: Kingswood Books, 2002), 35.

8. W. Reginald Ward and Richard P. Heitzenrater, eds., *The Works of John Wesley*, vol. 20: *Journals and Diaries III*, 1743–54 (Nashville: Abingdon Press,1991), 176–177.

9. W. Reginald Ward and Richard P. Heitzenrater, eds., *The Works of John Wesley*, vol. 23 (Nashville: Abingdon Press, 1995), 340.

10. Richard P. Heitzenrater, ed., *The Poor and the People Called Methodists 1729–1999* (Nashville: Kingswood Books, 2002), 230.

11. Ibid., 223

12. Ibid., 233.

13. Ibid., 228. All three clinics closed within a decade, as demand outstripped donations.

14. Ibid., 229

15. "Thoughts on the Present Scarcity of Provisions," in *The Works of John Wesley*, vol. 11, Jackson edition (Grand Rapids: Baker Book House, 1979).

16. Ibid., 55–56.

17. Ibid., 58–59.

18. Heitzenrater, *The Poor and the People Called Methodists*, 62.

19. Ibid., 62.

20. "The Use of Money," in *The Works of John Wesley*, vol. 2: *Sermons II*, ed. Albert C. Outler (Nashville; Abingdon Press, 1985), 266.

21 Ibid., 279.

22. Richard P. Heitzenrater, *Wesley and the People Called Methodists* (Nashville: Abingdon Press, 1995), 310–311.

23. "The Appeals to Men of Reason and Religion," 106.

24. "The New Creation," in *The Works of John Wesley*, vol. 2: *Sermons II*, ed. Albert C. Outler (Nashville: Abingdon Press, 1985), 504, 508, 509.

25. In the Introduction to John Wesley and Charles Wesley, *Hymns and Sacred Poems* (London: William Strahan, 1739).

26 "Upon Our Lord's Sermon on the Mount," Discourse IV, Sermon 24, in *John Wesley's Sermons: An Anthology*, eds. Albert C. Outler and Richard P. Heitzenrater (Nashville: Abingdon Press, 2008), 195.

27. W. Reginald Ward and Richard P. Heitzenrater, eds., *The Works of John Wesley*, vol. 21: *Journals and Diaries IV, 1755–65* (Nashville: Abingdon Press, 1992), 466.

28. "The Nature, Design, and General Rules of Our United Societies," *The Book of Discipline of The United Methodist Church*, 2008 (Nashville: Abingdon Press, 2008), ¶103.

29. Ibid., 73

30. Ibid., 73.

31. From the Charles Wesley Papers collection, Methodist Archives, John Rylands Library, University of Manchester, England. MS Luke: Charles Wesley, Box II.C.19.

32. M. Douglas Meeks, ed., *The Portion of the Poor* (Nashville: Kingswood Books, 1995), 63.

33. George H. Freeman, "From the General Secretary," World Methodist Council, worldmethodistcouncil.org.

34. Russell E. Richey, Kenneth E. Rowe, and Jean Miller Schmidt, *The Methodist Experience in America: A History*, vol. 1 (Nashville: Abingdon Press, 2010), 225.

35. See Theodore W. Jennings, *Good News to the Poor: John Wesley's Evangelical Economics* (Nashville: Abingdon Press, 1990). The Oxford Institute of Methodist Theological Studies devoted the ten-day gathering of scholars from around the world to Wesley and the poor. Lectures and papers from this conference were published in *The Portion of the Poor*, edited by M. Douglas Meeks (Nashville: Kingswood Books, 1995). Other scholars who have highlighted this dimension of our heritage are Jose Miguez Bonino, Ted Campbell, Joerg Rieger, Pamela Couture, Richard Heitzenrater, Randy Maddox, and M. Douglas Meeks.

36. The Council of Bishops of The United Methodist Church, *Children and Poverty: An Episcopal Initiative* (Nashville: The United Methodist Publishing House, 1996), 7.

37. See Dana L. Robert, *Joy to the World: Mission in the Age of Global Christianity, A Mission Study for 2010 and 2011* (New York: Women's Division, the General Board of Global Ministries, The United Methodist Church, 2010).

38. *Ministry with the Poor Guiding Principles and Foundations: Answering Jesus' Call to Discipleship in God's Mission of Love and Justice*, Interagency Task Force on Ministry with the Poor, The United Methodist Church, October 29, 2010, http://new.gbgm-umc.org/media/pdf/110209dlwithprinciples.pdf.

39. Heitzenrater, *The Poor and the People Called Methodists*, 36.

40. Ibid., 38.

Activists disrupt the opening of the 2010 International AIDS Conference in Vienna, Austria, on July 18. Several hundred demonstrators protested cutbacks in funding for AIDS care, treatment and prevention by U.S. and some European governments. (Paul Jeffrey)

Chapter 4

Poverties in the United States

Pamela D. Couture

From the admonition in the Old Testament to care for "widows, orphans, and strangers" to the admiration in the Book of Acts for the church that "held all things in common, and no one had need," biblical passages have reminded Christians of their responsibility for alleviating poverty. The Wesleyan movement embraced this concern by creating community centers where destitute people could access education, medical care, or employment. Members of United Methodist Women and its predecessor organizations have continued this heritage. Whether creating settlement houses in the late nineteenth century or calling attention to the plight of women and children in globalized economic structures in the late twentieth century, United Methodist Women foremothers have documented poverty and responded to poor people where they exist.

When members of United Methodist Women come face to face with poverty in their own communities, it is wise to begin with a "contextual analysis." The kind of community in which one lives determines how one best studies poverty in the United States. Experiencing poverty close to home is more difficult than away from home—poverty near our own home evokes different emotions than poverty overseas. So before beginning a study, sit quietly and meditate on these questions: What are my previous experiences with poverty? What visceral feelings does it create for me? Does my current neighborhood seem to be economically segregated, so that few poor people are evident? When I look at an environment, what clues suggest that poverty is more or less present?

When you are ready to continue, this chapter will lead you through the following questions:
1. What is the church's relationship to poverty in the United States? Is your congregation a church "for the poor" or "of the poor"?
2. What is poverty and who is responsible for eradicating it?
3. How is poverty calculated in the United States? What do we need to think about when we hear or read statistics about poverty?
4. How do we think about poverty in relation to children, women, men, ethnic minority persons, and communities?
5. What does the Church do?
6. In a changing society and economy, how do we keep current on information regarding poverty in the United States?[1]

A Church for the Poor or of the Poor?

As in the original Methodist movement, women are not only "caring with" people who are poor. Many women *are* "the poor." Women live in different kinds of poverty. For this reason, I speak not of poverty but of poverties.[2] Women live in historically poor Native American, African-American, or immigrant communities, in inner-city communities that have lost their manufacturing base, and in rural communities that have been depopulated by changes in agriculture. Women among the poor may be undocumented seasonal workers, married citizens of the United States who, with their husbands, work full time at minimum wage, or single parents. While The United Methodist Church in the United States since the nineteenth century has become bourgeois, a largely upwardly mobile, middle- and upper-middle-class church,[3] this should not obscure the reality that even here in The United Methodist Church in the United States, the real experts on poverty, those who live within arm's reach of it, are often already within our congregations.

The stereotypical "poor person" stands on the street corner with a cardboard sign, asking for food or a job. Such persons represent a spiritual "thorn in the flesh" for many Christians: the sign holders have learned to respond to anger or disdain with the words "God bless you." Occasionally one such person wanders into United Methodist congregations whose dominant economic ethos is well-to-do. For example, at Cathedral of the Rockies in downtown Boise, Idaho, the congregation mounted a multimillion dollar capital campaign to pay off the debt on its building. A homeless man in the service found the campaign organizers and gave a dollar, adding his name to the roster of donors who sought to secure the building for future generations.

In some congregations, however, an ethos of poverty dominates and wealth is the exception. At the Grand Avenue Temple in Kansas City, Missouri, the congregation is largely homeless, and the ministries respond to persons who are chronically poor.

In the 1960s Grand Avenue Temple, once a flourishing downtown "social gospel" church, declined in membership to a handful of members. Always a congregation "for the poor," it re-created itself as a congregation "of the poor" in which chronically homeless persons worship and access a variety of services, including food, clothing, medical care, and emergency shelter. Formerly homeless persons lead many of these ministries, offering dignity, encouragement, and respect. Grand Avenue's mission statement is recited each Sunday: "Grand Avenue Temple: Where Everybody is Somebody Special, Reaching Out to Unite All in God's love."

Grand Avenue Temple is filled with people who fit the stereotypes of *chronic* poverty—the homeless, the addicted, the mentally ill, the formerly incarcerated, or the undocumented economic refugee. But the majority of poor people—the hungry, the unemployed, the legal immigrant, the recently divorced or widowed, those fleeing from violence in the home, or those struggling to get an education—experience a different kind of poverty, *temporary poverty*. Most "poor people" have "spells" of poverty of three or four months, and sometimes these spells repeat themselves. Many people cannot meet their basic needs for a period of time in one or another area such as food, housing, clothing, medical and dental care, child care, and supervision; some spend many years hovering around the poverty threshold, the income guideline used to set policy for poverty-related programs, an amount established each year by the federal government.

We as the church may fail to recognize that poor persons are already among us in our congregations because many economically poor persons, especially women—such as women who claim the earned income tax credit on their tax return, women whose children are eligible for subsidized or free school lunches, women who use WIC (Supplemental Nutrition Program for Women, Infants, and Children) coupons at the grocery store, women who cannot get medical insurance—look like everyone else in the communities in which they live. Sometimes, people who qualify as "poor" are the pastors of our congregations. Sometimes, they wear uniforms and are enlisted in our armed services. They blend with the "nonpoor" community. And this is the way it should be. Many people who are poor are not eager to be identified as such, as they are easily stigmatized.

When a group of Methodists gather to study "poverty" or "poverties," the tendency is to refer to the poor as "them," as if the church belongs to "us," the dominant middle and upper-middle class. How will you, in your study group, create language that recognizes that poor people may be among you at the same time respecting the group's privacy about their personal circumstances, regardless of income level?

Over the years, United Methodist Women has traversed these sensitive boundaries in search of what Josiah Royce and Martin Luther King Jr. called the "beloved community." Led by research at the Women's Division of the United Methodist General Board of Global Ministries, the policymaking body of United Methodist Women, many groups have had the eyes to see where opportunity is limited by the United States' economic structure, to hear the cry of those who are in need in a community who may be ignored by others, and to welcome the Christ who is found in the neighbor. Members have been able to peer through a thicket of obstacles to see the God-created persons who struggle in the most affluent country in the world.

How will United Methodist Women take this heritage into the future and speak to those who are surprised by or intimidated by poverty in and beyond the church? How can members speak to the idea that embracing poverty and poor people in the United States, being a church "for the poor" and "of the poor," is a core value of the United Methodist Church, biblically and theologically?

What Is Poverty?

How is poverty spoken of in public, in political debates or in the news media? The concept of "poverty" suggests that an environment is insufficient to meet minimal standards to sustain human life. "Poor people," on the other hand, may live in abundant surroundings but cannot access the resources to meet minimal standards for living. Many different environments, and many different circumstances that lead to poverty, suggest that "poverties" exist in the United States.

What environments do people need to survive and to flourish? As part of the animal kingdom, people need water, food, shelter, and human comfort. As human beings, however, they need clothing, education, assistance during disease, and ways of organizing their communities—for worship, art, music, economic exchange—so that their goals and visions of flourishing can be met.

Poverty is usually associated with inadequate money. Poverty may also be about a place that lacks the goods and services that money represents; for example, many of the rural counties in the United States do not have a doctor or dentist to treat the local population. Or poverty may be about people who cannot get goods and services that are available because they have nothing to trade in return. At what point, then, is a person, a community, or a country considered poor because it lacks either money, goods, or services?

Poverty is a relative term, a "social construction" that expresses the way a society evaluates what people need not only to survive but to live according to the expectations and minimal requirements of that society. What we deem as "poverty" has to do with commonly held social expectations. What makes a person "poor" differs from one place to another.

In some places, people may be economically poor if they do not have land or skill to cultivate food or build a house; in other places, they may be poor if they do not have money to purchase food at the grocery market or rent clean, habitable shelter. In a complex society such as the United States some people would consider persons poor if they do not have access to primary, secondary, or university education, to preventive or curative medical or dental care, to multiple changes of clothing and shoes, or to employment, either by working for others or by accessing credit to start a small business. Therefore, we speak of "absolute" poverty and "relative" poverty. In absolute poverty people cannot obtain what they need to survive; in relative poverty people cannot attain the minimal social expectations in a given society. As social expectations change, the "standard of living" and "relative" poverty is modified.

Why does relative poverty hurt? A first-grade child who goes to school hungry because her family does not have enough food may be eligible for free or subsidized school lunch. She picks up her brown paper bag with her wrapped peanut butter sandwich, chips, carrot sticks and milk. It is the same lunch as all of the other children with brown bag lunches. She sits next to her friend who brings a shiny, Hello Kitty lunch box from home. The lunch box is filled with treats the friend most likes: snack packs, raisins, cheese and crackers, fruit rolls, and cookies. Every day she sees her friend with the shiny lunch box eat her favorite foods while her institutional brown bag lunch is ho-hum. Her friend eats with relish while, embarrassed by the brown bag, she picks at her lunch. But she eats.

She might not have much dinner at home. Already the children are learning about relative poverty and relative wealth.

Who Is Responsible for Eradicating Poverty?

What standard should be upheld for all, and who is responsible for upholding that standard—the individual, the family, the community as represented by civic groups and churches, or society as represented by government? This question has been debated since the founding of the United States.

Many economic refugees who settled the United States, people who were poor in their countries of origin, hoped that the land available in the United States would allow them to meet their basic needs by their own toil. The founders of the United States believed that the New World could overcome the poverty of the Old World. They knew that what we now call "structural issues"—laws and policies that organize society—made it difficult for individuals and families to succeed. In the early days of this nation, lawmakers eliminated structures that they saw as producing poverty, such as primogeniture, the inheritance law that concentrated land and wealth in the hands of the oldest son while leaving other children penurious. They established new, poverty-resisting structures, such as libraries and public education, believing these to be critical to overcoming poverty.[4] Even though policies and programs were created to resist poverty, some people couldn't find food and shelter for themselves. They needed assistance from their local community. Early on, the idea that a person seeking "poor relief" needed to do so in his or her own community took root. Precedent came from medieval Britain. As the feudal system broke down under fourteenth century globalization, British "poor laws" were established beginning in 1536. These laws determined where a person could seek relief and differentiated between those "deserving" of community care and those who were "undeserving." These distinctions became incorporated into early U.S. community policies.

The idea that the community should provide care for poor persons has theological roots in treatises such as Martin Luther's "Ordinance of a Common Chest (1523)."[5] The idea that the church should step in, providing both direct aid and access to a means of livelihood, infused the eighteenth century Wesleyan movement. The way that the founding fathers in the United States sought to overcome poverty reflected theological conversations that existed at the time.

The early reforms in the United States, however, did not specifically provide for Native Americans, slaves, women, or children. Almost a century after the founding of the United States, former slaves were finally granted legal rights as citizens, even though local and regional laws and customs often circumscribed those rights. Well after slavery formally ended, treaties with Native American tribes were broken again and again, destroying the culture and identity of native persons, until laws changed in the late twentieth century. A century and a half after the founding of the United States, women began to accrue the economic independence that gave them security apart from male control. After the Society for the Prevention of Cruelty to Animals was created, children, too, began to receive assistance when they were subjected to violence at home. Extending the poverty-resisting structures to persons other than white landowners took hold slowly.

The idea that the federal government in the United States should actively provide support for poor persons took hold in response to the needs of veterans after the Civil War. The aphorism that men laid down their lives on the battlefield and women did so in childbirth provided the rationale for the first national support for veterans and mothers.[6] During this era, the Methodist movement built community institutions—settlement houses, schools, orphanages, and hospitals—that greatly improved the resources available to poor people.

After the Great Depression of the 1930s created a national poverty of 25 percent, federal government officials, many of them influenced by the social gospel of the major protestant denominations,[7] expanded government social assistance to mothers, families, veterans, and the elderly through the development of Old-Age, Survivors and Disability Insurance. After World War II, veteran's assistance such as home mortgage and education assistance made it possible for many families in the United States to move from poor origins to more stable economic means of "the middle class."

This history shows that the debates we currently hear on our iPods, smartphones, televisions, and radios about what poverty is and the extent to which individuals, families, community organizations, or governments are responsible for it has deep roots in our national and ecclesial history. Our ideas about absolute and relative poverty—what we believe is enough—are constantly shifting. And the church of Jesus Christ has always participated in setting the norms for the "standard of living" and being part of the action creating access to that standard.

In light of the fact that our ideas about poverty are in constant flux, international thinking about poverty informs the discussion, even in the United States. Martha Nussbaum, studying women in India, has identified a series of needs that, "once given, women are loath to give up," arguing that these provide the foundation for the basic "capabilities" that women want. Nussbaum and Amaryta Sen, who contribute to the United Nations Development Report, have argued that the role of larger social groups—communities and governments—is to provide conditions in which all women and men have "capabilities," that they can exercise choices that allow them "to be and to do."[8] Contributing to the conversation that decides what environment the government and churches in the United States should create in order to support capabilities is as relevant in the United States as in any other part of the world. As we as a nation and as a church makes these decisions, we shape our national and ecclesial character. We determine what it means not only "to make disciples of Jesus Christ" but "to *be* disciples of Jesus Christ."

How Is Poverty Calculated in the United States?

In the United States the first "poverty threshold"—the anticipated income level around which people are likely not to be able to meet minimum needs—was established by the Department of Agriculture (USDA) in 1963. It calculated the quantity and presence of poverty in the United States based on a formula that estimated what would now be called a family's "food security." Then, a nonfarm family generally spent a third of its income on food. The USDA determined that a family could not care for its basic needs with less than three times the cost of a minimal diet. Official poverty statistics still calculate percentages of officially poor people in the United States on the basis of the cost of food.

In the past half century, however, the structure of the economy has changed. Nonfarm family expenditures on food have decreased to about 9.4 percent in 2010,[9] but the cost of housing, medical care, and child care has become a much larger portion of the family budget.[10] It is widely recognized that the former measurement no longer accurately reflects basic human requirements. Therefore, community and federal policies are often based on guidelines that are 140 to 200 percent above the official "poverty threshold." In this way government programs recognize that poverty in the United States is far greater than the official statistics suggest.

While policies that create eligibility above the poverty threshold respond to genuine human need, adjusting these percentages allows a municipality, county, or state to balance its budget. When I lived in Rochester, New York, child care subsidies were available to families with incomes at 200 percent of the poverty threshold and below. After the World Trade Center attacks in New York City, the entire budget of the state as well as allocations to local communities felt the economic shock. Monroe County, where Rochester is located, needed to cut its budget. One of the ways it could do this was by changing the percentage of poverty threshold at which families were eligible for subsidized care to 140 percent. The cuts were sudden and controversial. Poverty activists believed these responses to the budget shortfall were shortsighted, producing more costs in the long run. Early childhood quality care and education have long been proven to yield social benefits in behavior and ability to achieve a stable life later.[11] Stories of reconciling human need and governmental budget need can be found in almost every local news outlet today.

Some research think tanks, such as the National Center for Children and Poverty at Columbia University, use their own formulas to estimate poverty that take into account the change in the cost of different necessities and the assistance that families receive from local and federal governments. Few formulas in the United States, however, are sophisticated enough to estimate the substantial difference in the cost of living from one place to another. Major metropolitan areas are usually significantly higher in cost of living than towns or rural areas. While salaries of middle- and upper-middle-class people may rise with the cost of living in different regions, the minimum wages of lower paid workers are closer in range and often do not reflect these differences. And yet, high cost of living areas may be exactly where the minimum wage jobs are available. Therefore, many people in metropolitan areas whose income hovers below 200 percent of the poverty threshold pay increased prices that are not offset by the income they receive. Yet many people in rural areas may have fewer services to access and fewer job opportunities.

In the United States a major shift in the expectations of poor mothers occurred in 1997 with the change from Aid to Families with Dependent Children (AFDC) to Temporary Assistance for Needy Families (TANF). AFDC, and its predecessor, Aid to Dependent Children (ADC), established in 1935, was based on the premise that poor mothers should be able to stay at home to raise their children as middle-class mothers married to a man earning a family wage were able to do. As women were accepted into paid employment and as the number of single-parent mothers increased, the assumption of U.S. society changed from one of supporting mothers staying at home with children to supporting mothers' return to the workplace as quickly as possible after the birth of a child. The TANF program limited assistance after childbirth and assumed that a poor mother needed to develop workplace skills and find gainful employment. Once this assumption was established in law and policy, the mantra of think tanks who recommend changes in U.S. policy to reduce poverty became "make work pay!"

The United States seeks to "make work pay" by using tax law to reduce poverty rather than raising the minimum wage or creating social support programs such as the family allowances one finds in European countries. One effort to "make work pay" did significantly reduce the number poor families. The expansion of the earned income tax credit (EITC) in 1996 reduced the numbers of families and children who were officially poor. The EITC provides a tax rebate to a family that can file taxes but whose income is below a certain level.

TANF, on the other hand, has reduced dependence on government support programs but has not reduced poverty.[12] This program specified work requirements for families, but the minimum wages of many persons moving "from welfare to work" did not allow two-parent families working full time at minimum wage to rise above the federally established poverty threshold. After this program was introduced, the rise in poverty came not among government recipients of aid but among "the working poor"—parents who worked full time at minimum wage jobs but were still not able to rise above the poverty threshold.

This legislation provided another turning point for the population of impoverished persons in the United States: it made it clear which categories of people were likely to move into stable work and which were not. People with mental illness and drug addiction were not likely to become stable workers. Work that did not pay enough increased the ranks of families with children depending on shelters and food banks.

Furthermore, while poverty itself is not formally criminalized as it was in the 1800s when poor people were sent to the "workhouse," those conditions that create people's chronic inability to maintain stable employment often lead people to prison. In particular, mental illness and drug addiction plague people who cannot stabilize employment and have criminal histories. Furthermore, when persons are released from incarceration, they often remain poor, but they become ineligible for many of the government programs designed to help poor people stabilize their lives. If they live with family members, those persons also become ineligible for government assistance. Persons released from prison cannot access the kinds of social or familiar supports that most people use to stabilize their lives in times of stress.

These issues lie behind statistics on poverty and families, but children remain the largest subset of persons who are poor. While poverty in the United States among all people hovered from 11 percent in 1996 to a low of 8.7 percent in 2000 to a new high of 11.1 percent in 2009, the percentage of poor children dropped from 30 percent between 1996 and 2000 but has increased by 6 percent from 2000–2008.[13] Among poor children, the most vulnerable, as identified by the Annie E. Casey Foundation, are those children who are institutionalized in halfway homes or foster care, those children whose parents are incarcerated.[14]

Poverty in Relation to Children, Minorities, Women, and Communities

Children
Children make up the largest population of poor persons. According to the National Poverty Center at the University of Michigan, children make up 25 percent of the total population of the United States but 35 percent of the population that is officially poor.[15]

Native Americans, African Americans, and Hispanics
Native American, black, and Hispanic persons are disproportionately poor. In 2009, 25.8 percent of blacks and 25.3 percent of Hispanics were poor, compared to 9.4 percent of non-Hispanic whites and 12.5 percent of Asians. However, immigrants are a rising group of poor people. The National Poverty Center reports that in 2009, 19.0 percent of foreign-born persons were poor, as opposed to 13.7 percent of native-born persons. Foreign-born noncitizens have even higher rates of poverty: 25.1 percent.[16] The Annie E. Casey Foundation Kids Count database, one of the primary databases organizing and interpreting census data on child poverty and other indicators of child vulnerability and well-being, now tracks indicators for immigrant children.

Single-Parent Families Headed by Mothers
Children in single-parent families headed by mothers are more likely to be poor, especially if mothers are black or Hispanic. In 2009, 29.9 percent of families headed by a single mother was poor, in comparison to 16.9 percent of households headed by single men or 5.8 percent of households headed by a married couple.

In the 1990s the term "the feminization of poverty" highlighted the gendered aspects of poverty. "The feminization of poverty" was a term first used by Diana Pearce, a United Methodist in Evanston, Illinois, to describe the increasing rates of female poverty in inner-city neighborhoods in Chicago.[17] Lenore Weitzman then used the term to describe the declining financial security of mothers after divorce.[18] In both cases, the poverty of mothers was related to the absence of men who could be financial contributors to the household. In the inner city of Chicago, one-fourth of the men were likely to be dead or incarcerated by the time they were eighteen years old; in divorce, Weitzman argued, men were held less responsible for their previous wives and children as a result of no-fault divorce.

In *Blessed Are the Poor? Women's Poverty* and *Family Policy* I drew three conclusions about the reason that more mothers were likely to be poor, reasons applicable to both groups:

1. Women were more likely to be poor because earned less than men for the same work.
2. Women were more likely to be poor because they shared their lesser income with more dependents, diluting their ability to care fully for the needs of their families.
3. Women who came from historically poor communities were more likely to be poor.

Do these conclusions still hold?[19]

Gender Wage Gap

It continues to be true that women earn less than men. According to the U.S. Bureau of Labor Statistics, in the final quarter of 2010 across all occupations, women earned 81 percent of what their male counterparts earned. The gap between male and female earnings had closed most among African Americans, among whom women earned 96 percent of that of men, and was most wide among Asians, among whom women earned 75.9 percent compared to men.[20]

The Motherhood Penalty

Mothers, for a variety of reasons, have less money to distribute to more children. Sociologists at the University of Massachusetts now report the "motherhood penalty," a phenomenon in all but the highest income groups, in which mothers with more children earn significantly less than mothers with fewer children or than their childless counterparts, especially among lower income groups. In order to remedy this situation, sociologists encourage an increase in the EITC as well as increased subsidies for child care and early childhood education. These findings suggest that when mothers support their children alone, their money will need to stretch further than will the funds available to childless women, mothers of fewer children, or mothers whose children have multiple sources of support, as in a couple-headed family.[21]

Poverty Begets Poverty

A mother's poverty predicts her children's poverty; educate the mother and you help the child. Researchers at Cornell University have demonstrated that poverty at the time of a mother's birth correlates with lower birth weight for her children. The relationship between poverty and low birth weight translates into lower educational attainment and lower earnings.[22] Furthermore, when low-income mothers increase their education, their children's school performance increases and behavior problems decrease. Researchers at Northwestern University believe that children benefit directly, in terms of enrichment in the home, and indirectly from higher income and material well-being.[23] While most TANF welfare-to-work programs encourage "work first," the researcherrs suggest that an "education first" strategy might have more significant benefits in the long run.

What Does the Church Do?

The first question for United Methodists to ask is: What is my congregation or annual conference or United Methodist Women already doing with and for ministry among people who are poor, either in their volunteer lives or in their work lives? Who is serving, for example, as tutors or mentors for struggling children or formerly incarcerated persons, providing pro bono legal, nursing, or medical case, or assisting people who are creating small businesses? What programming currently exists within the community or within the church that should be buttressed? What new programming needs to be created?

Annual conference programs in the United States differ according to the needs and interests of people in their own contexts, for example:
- East Ohio Annual Conference and Southwest Texas, like Grand Avenue Temple, revitalized failing congregations as congregations of and for poor children.[24]

- North Carolina Annual Conference partnered congregations and schools.[25]
- New Jersey Annual Conference developed a tri-focus relationship with an African annual conference, an insurance company, and the State of New Jersey.[26]
- Desert Southwest Annual Conference created Sidewalk Sunday Schools.[27]
- Virginia and Wisconsin Annual Conferences created camps for children of incarcerated persons.[28]

Most congregations, communities, and annual conferences have more that is currently happening than people realize.

The second question to ask is: What is the effect in my community of changes in government at the federal, state, or local level? What effects has my community felt or will feel as changes occur in early childhood programming such as Head Start, Medicaid, Medicare, or other health system reforms? What is the role of United Methodist Women in highlighting the effects of social and denominational change on struggling people as these changes occur in the midst of concern for denominational decline and the national budget deficit?

Keeping Information Current in the United States

Three decades ago, when I began my studies of poverty in the United States and theology, the primary emerging analysis focused on gender, family structure, and ethnic minority communities. At that time, poverty in the United States was significantly higher than in European countries, and two factors—nationally available health insurance and federally collected child support—were credited with European countries' lower poverty rates. In the intervening years more women have entered employment, welfare laws now support paid work, and family laws and customs have changed so that fathers are more financially supportive and involved in their children's lives. Research data abounds on child care, early childhood education, mother's education, and changes in social attitudes toward family structure. Perhaps the most profound change has to do with data now being collected and made public about the poverty among new immigrant families. And new immigrants are but a reflection of the new version of a globalized economy in which money flows around the globe and people try to follow.

The following websites can assist study groups as they search to understand poverty in their own zip codes:
- Annie E. Casey Foundation Kid's Count Data Center: www.aecf.org
- National Center for Children in Poverty at Columbia University: www.nccp.org
- National Poverty Center at the University of Michigan: www.npc.umich.edu
- Institute for Policy Research at Northwestern University: www.northwestern.edu/ipr/research/respoverty1.html
- Harris School of Public Policy at the University of Chicago: harrisschool.uchicago.edu
- Institute for Research on Poverty at the University of Wisconsin–Madison: www.irp.wisc.edu
- University of Kentucky Center for Poverty Research: www.ukcpr.org
- Rural Policy Research Institute of the University of Missouri, University of Nebraska, and Iowa State University: www.rupri.org
- Stanford Center on Poverty an Inequality: www.stanford.edu/group/scspi

While statistics and trends are important, they cannot substitute for relationships, experiences, and stories that church people hear as we become acquainted with one another and with people in our own communities. A statistic should never obscure a human face; a trend should never circumscribe human potential. The theology of the Wesleyan movement is based on relationship—relationship with God, with seeing Christ in the face of the stranger, with ourselves as we decide what kind of communities we want to live in and what kind of people we want to be.

Notes

1. In the last years of the Bishops Initiative on Children and Poverty (1996–2004), I interviewed people in each of the Annual Conferences of The United Methodist Church about their ministries with "children and poverty." These stories, including names and annual conferences of the interviewees, many of whom are still available as resource people, can be found in the last three chapters of Pamela D. Couture, *Child Poverty: Love, Justice and Social Responsibility* (St. Louis: Chalice Press, 2007). In this chapter I will share my own observations of other exemplary persons and ministries who have created lasting images responding to poverty and the church in the United States.

2. Pamela D. Couture, *Blessed Are the Poor? Women's Poverty, Family Policy, and Practical Theology* (Nashville: Abingdon Press, 1991).

3. Donald Dayton, "Whither Evangelicalism?" in *Sanctification and Liberation: Liberation Theologies in Light of the Wesleyan Tradition*, ed. Theodore Runyon (Nashville: Abingdon Press, 1981), 152.

4. Thomas Jefferson, *Thomas Jefferson: Writings*, Library of America (New York: Literary Classics of the United States, 1984), 44.

5. Martin Luther, *Luther's Works*, vol. 45 (Philadelphia, Fortress Press, 1962), 161–194.

6. Theda Skocpol, *Protecting Soldiers and Mothers: The Political Origins of Social Policy in the United States* (Boston: Belknap Press, 1992), 7–11.

7. Christopher Evans, *The Kingdom Is Always But Coming: A Biography of Walter Rauschenbusch* (Waco, TX: Baylor University Press, 2010), xxiv.

8. Martha C. Nussbaum, *Women and Human Development: The Capabilities Approach* (Cambridge: Cambridge University Press, 2000), 4–14.

9. U.S. Department of Agriculture, Economic Research Service, "Food CPI and Expenditures, Table 7," updated July 13, 2011, www.ers.usda.gov/Briefing/CPIFoodAndExpenditures/Data/Expenditures_tables/table7.htm, accessed September 6, 2011.

10. Debra Pankow, "How Much Should We Spend?" North Dakota State University, revised June 2009, www.ag.ndsu.edu/pubs/yf/fammgmt/fe440w.htm, accessed September 6, 2011.

11. Donald Pryor, "Access to Subsidized Child Care in Monroe County, New York," Center for Governmental Research, September 2007, www.cgr.org/reports/07_R-1524_AccesstoSubsidizedChildCareinMC.pdf, accessed September 6, 2011.

12. See, for example, Michigan in Brief, "Welfare Reform: TANF Reauthorization," www.michiganinbrief.org/edition07/Chapter5/WelformReform.htm, accessed August 30, 2011: "Many people have left welfare only to join the ranks of the working poor." Also note increase in child care needs and applications for other social services.

13. Annie E. Casey Foundation, *Kids Count 2010 Data Book* (Baltimore, MD: Annie E. Casey Foundation), p. 12, datacenter.kidscount.org/DataBook/2010/OnlineBooks/2010DataBook.pdf, accessed May 25, 2011.

14. Pamela D. Couture, *Child Poverty: Love, Justice and Social Responsibility* (St. Louis: Chalice Press, 2007), 80.

15. National Poverty Center, "Poverty in the United States, Frequently Asked Questions," The National Poverty Center, University of Michigan, www.npc.umich.edu/poverty/#3, accessed May 25, 2011.

16. Ibid., accessed June 6, 2011.

17. Diana Pearce, "The Feminization of Poverty: Women, Work, and Welfare," *Urban and Social Change Review* 11 (1978): 28–36.

18. Lenore J. Weitzman, *The Divorce Revolution: The Unexpected Social and Economic Consequences for Women and Children in America* (New York: The Free Press, 1985).

19. Couture, *Blessed Are the Poor?*, 38–47.

20. U.S. Bureau of Labor Statistics, "Median Weekly Earnings for Men and Women in Fourth Quarter 2010," www.bls.gov/opub/ted/2011/ted_20110124.htm, accessed June 6, 2011.

21. American Sociological Association, "Sociologists Find Lowest-Paid Women Suffer Most from Motherhood Penalty," October 5, 2010, www.asanet.org/press/motherhood_penalty.cfm, accessed October 11, 2011.

22. Janet Currie and Enrico Morietti, "Biology as Destiny? Short and Long Run Determinants of Birthweight," August 2005, www.econ.ucla.edu/people/papers/currie/more/IGC_aug05.pdf, accessed June 5, 2011.

23. Karen A. Magnusen and Sharon M. McGroder, "The Effect of Increasing Welfare Mothers' Education on Their Young Children's Academic Problems and School Readiness," Joint Center for Poverty Research at Northwestern University and Chicago University, www.northwestern.edu/ipr/jcpr/workingpapers/wpfiles/magnuson_mcgroder.pdf, accessed June 6, 2011.

24. Couture, *Child Poverty*, 182, 185–186.

25. Ibid., 183.

26. Ibid., 184.

27. Ibid., 185.

28. Ibid., 186–187.

A Honduran girl in the doorway of her adobe house. *(Paul Jeffrey)*

Chapter 5

Global Poverty: We're All Connected

David Wildman

Today roughly half of the world's population, over three billion of our sisters and brothers, live in poverty, on less than $2.50 per day. Half of all humanity is not able to meet its daily basic needs of food, water, clothing, shelter, and health care. The human toll of such deprivation is enormous. Roughly one-third of all human deaths each year are due to poverty-related causes; this translates into some 50,000 deaths each day from largely preventable causes. People die from lack of adequate nutrition, from lack of clean water and sanitation, from lack of access to medical care, clothing, shelter, and education. One analyst, Thomas Pogge, observed that "many more people—some 360 million—have died from hunger and remediable diseases in peacetime, in the twenty years since the end of the Cold War than perished from wars, civil wars, and government repression over the entire twentieth century."[1]

Yet the modern global economy has also generated tremendous wealth in the past twenty years. How can so many be dying and in want in a context of such abundance? Why are we as a world community failing to meet the needs of our impoverished neighbors? Part of the answer lies in the growing inequality in the accumulation and consumption of resources. Over the same twenty years, the gap between the rich and the poor has become wider than ever, both within nations and between so-called developed nations of the north and so-called developing nations of the global south.

Is global poverty today simply a result of some people being less willing to share resources than previous generations? How do we find better ways to redistribute global resources so that all may have enough? Is there something in the way our global economy produces wealth that impoverishes whole communities and generates widespread poverty? What role are churches playing in the efforts of impoverished communities around the world to meet their basic needs? These are some of the questions this chapter seeks to address.

Defining Poverty: Asking the Wrong People the Wrong Question

The neoliberal economic theory of the World Bank and International Monetary Fund (IMF) is based on a definition of economic development solely in terms of increasing aggregate income and wealth. If the economy of a nation grows, so this line of thinking goes, then there will be more income for all. In today's global economy, the theory assumes that the fastest way to generate income is through trade—especially trade for export. Throughout the 1980s and 1990s, World Bank and IMF policies pushed one developing nation after another to shift from local agricultural production to production for export. While the overall gross domestic product (GDP) of many countries went up, much of the wealth went to government officials, corporations, and wealthy landowners. The rising GDP per capita of countries like the Philippines masked the devastating impact these policies had on small farmers and rural communities.

Only by defining poverty at an extremely low level of $1.00 per day (recently raised to $1.25 per day) can they claim that extreme income poverty has gone down slightly. Yet in recognition of their low poverty level, most World Bank studies include data on the number of people with incomes below $2.00 per day or $2.50 per day, which shows an increase in the number who are poor.

In 1990, the United Nations Development Program (UNDP) launched a new report and a new measurement called "the Human Development Index" (HDI) that sought to define human development in terms of qualities of life rather than simply by income or GDP per capita. The HDI tried to quantify qualities like literacy rates, life expectancy, and under-five mortality rates. Each year the Human Development Report examined quantitative data on a different quality of life and created additional indexes like the Human Poverty Index and the Gender Development Index. The HDI came up with a measure that ranked each nation, though it was still aggregate data for the whole country and not broken down by different sectors of society. Muhbub ul Haq, one of the founders of the HDI, expressed the limits of any such economic statistics in conveying the realities of poverty facing so many: "Beware of statistics: if half your body is in an oven and half your body is in a freezer, then on average you are comfortable when in fact every part of you is hurting!"[2] While the Human Development Reports convey a better quantitative portrait of development and poverty in each nation, they fail to address the impact of global economic policies on poor communities.

Removing the Log in Our Own Eye in Addressing Global Poverty

Why do you see the speck in your neighbor's eye, but do not notice the log in your own eye?

— Matthew 7:3

In the fall of 1990, the same year that UNDP launched its Human Development Report, several key events occurred that embodied contradictory approaches to ending global poverty. The UN held a World Summit for Children in New York that was, at the time, the largest gathering of heads of state, and this quickly led to the adoption of the International Convention on the Rights of the Child. To this day this convention is the most widely adopted human rights treaty in the world, with only the United States refusing to ratify it. It offers a framework for government commitments and actions that would end child poverty.

During the summit and immediately thereafter, then U.S. Secretary of State James Baker met with many heads of state and traveled the globe to raise seventy billion dollars. Tragically, all of that money was used to wage war against Iraq and to restore Kuwait's monarchy. The United States raised not one cent for programs promoting the well-being of children.

Many had hoped with the end of the Cold War in 1989 that there would be a peace dividend that could redirect resources from military spending into programs eradicating poverty. However, the United States, Russia, and other cold war nations sought to sell more and more arms to authoritarian regimes with impoverished populations. The Nigerian ambassador to the UN described the impact of the end of the cold war on peoples of the global south with a Swahili proverb: "When two elephants fight, the grass gets trampled." For decades the two elephants (superpowers) had been fighting, and the grass (global south) kept getting trampled. He then added that when two elephants make love, the grass also gets trampled. As governments and companies East and West sought to build new trade relations over the next twenty years, communities in the global south found their lives repeatedly ground down like the grass.

Hunger, Food Security, and the Struggle for Food Sovereignty

They shall build houses and inhabit them; they shall plant vineyards and eat their fruit. They shall not build and another inhabit; they shall not plant and another eat; for like the days of a tree shall the days of my people be, and my chosen shall long enjoy the work of their hands.

— Isaiah 65:21–22

More than one billion people do not get enough to eat each day. While the number of people affected by hunger gradually declined from 1970–1996 from 880 million to 825 million, the number suffering from hunger has risen dramatically since then. From 1996–2009, the number of people facing hunger grew by nearly 25 percent to more than one billion. Almost all live in India, sub-Saharan Africa, and the rest of Asia. One in four of those who hunger are children. Half are small farmers, 20 percent are rural landless, and 10 percent are pastoralists and fishing and forest communities, while the remaining 20 percent are urban poor.[3]

It is striking that 80 percent of those who hunger live and work in food-producing areas. Far too many people today plant crops, raise livestock, and catch fish that someone else will eat. The problem is not a lack of resources; there is enough arable land and enough food production to provide adequate nutrition for all people. The problem is a global economic system that denies so many people the fruits of their labors.

Give a person a fish and he or she eats for a day; teach a person to fish and he or she will eat for a lifetime. For years churches have used this simple saying to shift our approach toward global hunger and poverty from charity to capacity building—helping people help themselves. Yet to get at some of the root causes of impoverishment we need to take this saying further. Global trade policies today in effect insist that fishing lessons are available only if a community agrees to export all the fish it catches. Communities are pressured into converting rice paddies into shrimp farms—again for export—that concentrates waste and increases risk of disease. Such fish farming often becomes inoperable after several years, and the land remains infertile for some time. When that happens, companies move on, but people suffer. Overfishing, pollution, and dying coral reefs have pushed fishing further offshore requiring expensive boats to continue.

Bangladesh, Sweatshops, Walmart, and the Right to Organize

And though one might prevail against another, two will withstand one. A threefold cord is not quickly broken.

— Ecclesiastes 4:12

The best preventive medicine against poverty is the right of workers, farmers, and communities to organize. If we take a moment to read the labels on our clothes, the food we eat, and all the products we use each day, many of us will discover that we are a walking united nations with resources from many places around the world. We know about where goods come from, how much they cost, and the quality of products. But do we know anything about the quality of life for the workers who made them? Ending global poverty will involve building relationships with our sisters and brothers and getting to know something about their lives.

Walmart is one of the biggest retailers in the world. As such it commands enormous power to set prices on various products simply by the volume of its purchases. In effect, Walmart can pit factories in Central America, Bangladesh, Vietnam, and China against one another as it presses for the lowest price on goods. These low prices come at a high cost to workers in terms of unsafe working conditions, long hours, and low wages.[4]

Some of the worst labor conditions in the garment industry are in Bangladesh. Numerous fires and building collapses have killed scores of workers. Wages are among the lowest of any garment-producing country. Labor leaders and workers who try to organize routinely face harassment and even arrest. In August 2010, three leaders with the Bangladesh Center for Worker Solidarity (BCWS), Kalpona Akter, Babul Akhter, and Aminul Islam, were all arrested on false charges of inciting violence by the government.

With companies organizing and operating globally, workers need to organize globally as well. This is just what BCWS did. BCWS mobilized support from International Labor Rights Forum (ILRF), Human Rights Watch, and other international partners to press the government to release the workers and investigate working conditions in the factories. In the spring of 2011, BCWS leaders came to the United States and joined in the 100th anniversary commemoration in New York of the Triangle shirtwaist fire in which dozens of immigrant garment workers died. The Triangle fire put pressure on the local city government to adopt fire safety regulations to protect workers. The Bangladeshi workers present shared their struggle for the same kinds of protections from fires in factories today.

With support from ILRF, the workers went on to meet with Walmart workers in the United States and to speak at the Walmart annual shareholder meeting, describing the horrendous conditions and low wages they face in the very factories that provide many garments to Walmart. These global organizing efforts by BCWS have led to a number of companies joining with human rights advocates in demanding better conditions and wages.

Instead of a race to the bottom that pits workers against one another, there is now a global movement toward raising working conditions and wages in Bangladesh, Central America, China, and wherever workers are exploited. Next time we shop for clothes let us each check the label, and also check with ILRF[5] to hear from workers like Kalpona, Babul, and Aminul. Each time we organize together, we will make a difference.

Uzbekistan: Cotton, Poverty, and Child Labor

Listen! The wages of the laborers who mowed your fields, which you kept back by fraud, cry out, and the cries of the harvesters have reached the ears of the Lord of hosts.

— James 5:4

Each fall as many as one to two million Uzbek schoolchildren do not go back to school to study but are forced back into the fields to pick cotton. Whole schools are given quotas by their repressive government, and teachers are threatened if they do not meet the quota. Uzbekistan is the sixth largest producer of cotton and the third largest cotton exporter in the world. The cotton harvest, picked entirely by hand, generates over one billion dollars in profits for the country's brutal dictator, Islam Karimov, and a few elites closely allied with him.

Human rights groups, both Uzbek and international, have documented widespread use of child labor in cotton production for several years. They concluded that child labor in the Uzbek cotton harvest is not the result of poverty as in other countries where children are forced to work to supplement family income. Rather, the *forced* labor of children, teachers, and many others for little or no wages impoverishes many families.[6] The harsh conditions of handpicking cotton—long hours in the hot sun, drinking unclean water from irrigation pipes, exposure to high levels of pesticides, and forcing children to miss several months of school each year—combined with a climate of fear and government repression all amount to a modern day sharecropping system that locks whole communities into destitution from one generation to the next.

As more and more land goes to highly profitable cotton production, there is less land for local food production. Across Central Asia, cotton-producing regions have disproportionately higher rates of poverty and malnutrition. Cotton production causes widespread water depletion as well. Most of the land devoted to cotton is irrigated, and aging irrigation systems have led to high rates of leakage. High amounts of leakage contribute to rising salinization of the soil as too much water leeches minerals to the surface where the water evaporates leaving a layer of salt. To reduce salinization and keep cotton yields from falling, many farms will "rinse" their fields, which uses even more water. Over the past 45 years the Aral Sea has declined in volume by more than 75 percent, and its once thriving fishing industry is largely gone. Crop rotation would replenish soil nutrients and allow greater food production but is rarely utilized as it cuts into the enormous profits the elite reap from forced cotton production.

With few options besides cotton, an increasing number of rural people migrate to cities and nearby Kazakhstan and Russia where even the low wages as day laborers may be more than they would get in a month picking cotton. Most migrant workers who leave to find work are men, so the burden of forced labor in cotton fields falls heaviest on women and children.

In the aftermath of the 9/11 attacks, the Uzbek government, in the name of the "war on terror," justified its repressive measures as necessary in fighting Islamic extremists. Yet the International Crisis Group report concluded, "In reality, the government's stance has much more to do with the economic exploitation that benefits a small elite. While an unfair economic system is in place, and farmers have no rights to land or land use, the government needs a repressive apparatus to ensure cotton continues to be grown. One result, ironically, will be more unemployed, impoverished young men, susceptible to Islamist ideologies."[7]

As the fall 2011 harvest season began and more than a million Uzbek children were again forced out into the fields, the Obama Administration met with Uzbek government officials in Washington, DC. The administration pushed to restore military aid to a brutal regime in order to facilitate increasing use of Uzbekistan as a supply route for the war in Afghanistan. Tragically, the United States placed greater value on the safe and free flow of goods through Uzbekistan for war than on the safety and freedom of impoverished Uzbek children subjected to forced labor.

The ILRF, a longtime United Methodist partner, has joined many other international human rights groups to support Uzbek women and children in challenging the Uzbek and U.S. governments and companies to end child labor and other forms of impoverishing forced labor.

Monsanto Genetically Modified Seeds Unwelcome in Haiti

They shall all sit under their own vines and under their own fig trees, and no one shall make them afraid.

— Micah 4:4

After the devastating earthquake in Haiti in January 2010, groups around the world pledged their desire to help impoverished Haitians. One of the organizations that offered to help was Monsanto. Monsanto is a giant U.S. chemical company that produces pesticides, herbicides, genetically modified organisms (GMOs), and hybrid seeds. They control roughly half of all seed patents.

Monsanto, working in cooperation with USAID, offered 475 tons of seed to Haiti—but they came with a catch. For millennia farmers have saved some seed from one season for the next season. Some of Monsanto's seeds were hybrids that would not reproduce in another season. Some were soaked in toxic chemicals that the U.S. Environmental Protection Agency declared unsafe for home gardening. Many Haitian farmers plant by hand. In addition, some GMO seeds would affect the overall biodiversity in Haiti and force farmers to buy the same seeds in future years. If seeds were donated or farmers could afford them such offerings might have been more welcome, but under this process poor farmers would soon be forced to go into debt to get GMO seeds that they had never needed before.

In June 2010, ten thousand peasant farmers marched in protest and even burned some of the Monsanto seeds. Chavannes Jean-Baptiste, head of the Peasant Movement of Papay, explained,

> Fighting hybrid and GMO seeds is critical to save our diversity and our agriculture. We have the potential to make our lands produce enough to feed the whole population and even to export certain products. The policy we need for this to happen is food sovereignty, where the county has a right to define its own agricultural policies, to grow first for the family and then for local market, to grow healthy food in a way which respects the environment and Mother Earth.[8]

For many who believe ending hunger is simply a matter of increasing food production and crop yields, GMO seeds can seem like an attractive answer. But across the globe the cost of GMO seeds, far from reducing poverty, has forced many small farmers who are unable to pay for seeds to lose their land to large landlords or to agribusiness. "People in the U.S. need to help us produce, not give us food and seeds. They're ruining our chance to support ourselves," said Haitian farmer Jonas Deronzil, who belongs to a rural peasant cooperative.[9]

Olivier De Shutter, the UN Special Rapporteur on the Right to Food, raises serious questions about GMO-based strategies. He observes,

> I don't see the exit strategy. I fear in the long term we will have developed a dependency on external inputs that the poorest farmers will not be able to afford, inputs whose prices will only become more expensive and volatile. It is in the name of boosting production that the scramble for natural resources is legitimized, that the push for more chemical agriculture is justified, and that small-scale farmers are pushed off the land, leading to more rural poverty and rural-to-urban migration.[10]

De Shutter lifts up *agroecology*—small-scale farming for local food consumption—as an alternative that outproduces the chemical dependent, high cost Western agriculture by reducing waste and the need for expensive transport. Citing a program established in Belo Horizonte, Brazil, he states, "By developing farmers' markets, community kitchens, programs to prepare food for the very poor and other initiatives, a new localized food system was rebuilt from the bottom up."

Conflict Minerals, Cell Phones, and the Democratic Republic of the Congo

In the abundance of your trade you were filled with violence, and you sinned.

— Ezekiel 18:16

The bloodiest war since World War II is the one that has enveloped much of the Democratic Republic of the Congo (DRC) from 1998–2002. More than six million died, and more than one million were internally displaced in one of the poorest countries that has rising rates of poverty and malnutrition. Yet the DRC is a land with many valuable resources: tin, tungsten, tantalum, and gold. How can such immense resource wealth coexist with such widespread poverty?

With the tremendous growth in the electronics industry and telecommunications, world demand for tin, tantalum, and tungsten has steadily increased. The global attention on "blood diamonds" from countries such as Sierra Leone that were torn by conflict fueled by cash from diamonds led a number of international human rights groups, combined with religious shareholders, to press companies and governments to address the violence and impoverishment associated with conflict minerals. The term *conflict minerals* refers to any minerals mined under control of armed groups and is primarily applied to the DRC and other countries in Africa. The easiest form of mining for militias to control and exploit are those of small-scale surface mining. In the DRC most of the mining is done by an estimated two million small-scale miners, most of whom come from poor local communities where the mining is done and have few other sources of income.

Minerals from the DRC cost roughly half that of other locations primarily because of the low wages. Miners in the DRC make from one to five dollars per day. With so many small mining operations spread across the country, armed groups have found it easy to make huge profits exploiting miners and the transport routes for getting minerals to market. Large amounts of cash in the hands of armed groups deepen the instability and impoverishment throughout the region.

The amount of tantalum used in a cell phone costs roughly fifty cents, so even doubling the wages of miners would do little to the overall cost of a phone. Efforts by human rights groups and shareholders have led some companies to develop monitoring mechanisms to trace the source and conditions of conflict minerals from the DRC. These efforts are critical, but they are only a first step in confronting the problem of conflict minerals and the impoverished communities from where they come. The fastest growing market for cell phones and other electronic goods is now in Asia, where there is not yet a strong commitment to human rights monitoring. The monitoring process also does not fully address issues of forced labor and exploitation in government-run mines but only those in areas where militias operate.[11]

Climate Change Devastates Impoverished Communities

Is it not enough for you to feed on the good pasture, but you must tread down with your feet the rest of your pasture? When you drink of clear water, must you foul the rest with your feet? And must my sheep eat what you have trodden with your feet, and drink what you have fouled with your feet?

— Ezekiel 34:18–19

The dynamics of climate change—rising ocean temperatures, desertification, increasing severity and number of storms, glacial melting—affect us all, but not all equally. The heaviest impact of climate change falls on some of the most impoverished nations, which, ironically, have among the lowest carbon emissions globally. For instance, more than 60 percent of Bangladesh's land is fewer than five meters above sea level, and as much as two-thirds can be submerged during times of flooding. Severe floods regularly damage crops and livestock, placing additional burdens on already impoverished communities.

Small island states are by far the most vulnerable. Some like Tuvalu and the Maldives may cease to exist in a few years. With rising sea levels, Tuvalu's groundwater has become increasingly salinized, reducing crop production and making access to fresh drinking water harder. The rising ocean temperatures have also led to dying of the coral reefs that surround the island. As a result, fish that thrived amid the coral are moving further offshore and islanders are losing a critical source of food and income.

Coral reefs play a major role in reducing storm surge impact on islands. As coral reefs die, they become brittle and lose their capacity to protect islands during storms, which accelerates land loss. Without dramatic and swift actions to reduce carbon emissions by the United States and other major energy consuming countries, the poor communities of small island states will soon become climate-change refugees.

At the same time, nearly half of Africa faces the risk of growing desertification from chronic and repeated droughts combined with widespread deforestation. In sub-Saharan Africa, 75 percent of agriculture is rain fed. Thus, severe and extended drought threatens widespread food shortages such as the current crisis in Somalia. As droughts persist, many poor communities are forced to migrate simply to survive, thereby creating further pressures on nearby areas with scarce water and food supplies.

Tragically, poor communities whose residents never used air-conditioning, drove a sport utility vehicle, or flew in a plane face loss of land, livelihood, and their lives in part due to overconsumption of fossil fuels by others. Long ago, the prophet Ezekiel warned that consumptive and wasteful lifestyles have an impact on the earth and on our neighbors and are displeasing to God. Efforts to create green congregations and reduce our carbon footprint will help restore relations with creation, with our neighbors far away, and with God.

Afghanistan: How War and Militarism Creates Poverty

So I said, "Wisdom is better than might; yet the poor man's wisdom is despised, and his words are not heeded." Wisdom is better than weapons of war, but one bungler destroys much good.

— Ecclesiastes 9:16, 18

One of the things war does well is destroy resources. It destroys lives, fields, factories, and homes. Likewise, military spending devotes precious resources toward destruction rather than creating productive capacity. The greatest victims of both war and military spending are poor communities. Those fighting and dying on the front lines are almost always poor and working class.

Most refugees and internally displaced persons (IDPs) today, who are especially vulnerable and impoverished, were forced to flee due to wars and conflict. More than half of today's uprooted are from countries where the United States has devoted billions in war spending, such as Afghanistan, Iraq, Pakistan, and Palestine.

Today the so-called war on terror constitutes one of the greatest threats to poor communities across the globe. The war on terror divides people by erecting walls of fear and silencing the truth about the relationships between resources and poverty. In the name of national security and homeland security, one government after another has redirected resources away from peoples' needs to serve the interests of the powerful.

What a difference it would make if governments turned their priorities from arms sales to building the capacity of farms and factories, schools, and health centers that enable people to meet their own needs. War and military spending, by destroying and diverting resources, create scarcity and competition over resources that tend to concentrate in the hands of a few at the expense of the many.

Afghanistan is one of the poorest countries in the world with one of the highest infant and maternal mortality rates. Each day 850 Afghan children die from largely preventable causes—lack of clean drinking water, diarrhea, malnutrition, tuberculosis. Most lived in remote, rural villages with limited education and primary health services. One in four Afghan children will not reach the age of five, and life expectancy is in the midforties. The U.S. government voiced tremendous concern for the lives of Afghans, especially Afghan women, and has pumped hundreds of billions of resources into the country since October 2001. However, 97 percent of U.S. resources devoted to Afghanistan were for weapons, U.S. soldiers, and military training. While the United States funded arms and training for several hundred thousand Afghan soldiers and police, the United States has trained fewer than two thousand Afghan women as midwives. After more than ten years of U.S. military presence and some five hundred billion dollars in resources, Afghan women and children remain among the most vulnerable and impoverished in the world.[12]

The United Methodist Social Principles point to a profoundly different way of engaging with Afghan communities and others long disrupted by war: "conflicts and war impoverish the population on all sides, and an important way to support the poor will be to work for peaceful solutions."[13] While the U.S. government has devoted huge amounts of resources to waging war, the United Methodist General Board of Global Ministries and other nongovernmental organizations have worked in partnership with impoverished communities in Afghanistan, the DRC, Liberia, Sierra Leone, and many other conflict areas to provide health care and basic education. These programs are like a few loaves and fish compared with the massive amounts of resources that today's empire devotes to war and militarism, yet they embody some of the most significant antipoverty programs today. Such small-scale programs are models of beating swords into plowshares so that poor rural communities may again live under their own vines and fig trees where no one will make them afraid (see Micah 4:3–4). It's time that we relearn the biblical lesson that antiwar movements are fundamentally antipoverty movements and vice versa.

Rebalancing Our Global Economy to End Poverty

I do not mean that there should be relief for others and pressure on you, but it is a question of a fair balance between your present abundance and their need, so that their abundance may be for your need, in order that there may be a fair balance. As it is written, "The one who had much did not have too much, and the one who had little did not have too little."

— 2 Corinthians 8:13–15

Global trade policies should serve people's needs, but too often people are forced to serve the interests of trade. The Bible affirms the goodness of trade and debt if they are used as tools for a community to share and distribute its resources more equitably so that no one becomes impoverished. Simply put, debt is a temporary reallocation of community resources to enable people to trade and do now what would otherwise not be possible. When debt serves people, it is a tool of empowerment. But when mounting debts force people to sell their land, their children, and their lives to serve the debt (as in today's debt crisis of small farmers and developing nations), then it becomes a tool of oppression and extortion.

The fifth chapter of Nehemiah describes how subsistence farmers are forced, in times of famine and drought, to trade their land and their labor just to get food to survive and to keep paying tribute (i.e., the king's tax) to the wealthy. Nehemiah categorically condemns such unjust trading practices that would strip family farmers of their land, which is not only a family heritage but their sole means of survival. "I brought charges against the nobles and the officials; I said to them, 'You are all taking interest from your own people. Restore to them, this very day, their fields, their vineyards, their olive orchards, and their houses, and the interest you have been exacting from them'" (Nehemiah 5:7, 11).

Trade enables communities across widespread areas to make use of produce, goods, and services from far away. Trade serves to enhance the quality of our lives and relationships. But is trade always good for everyone? Is more trade always better? It is a big stretch to assert that trade should be the sole model and measure of what is good in society. Wealthy traders in biblical days and neoliberal economic theorists today declare as unquestioned dogma that the ever-increasing quantities of trade (export-oriented trade in particular) should be the organizing principle and fundamental value for all decisions and relations in society. When trade is seen as a quantity of goods to be accumulated rather than a quality of relations within and between communities, it becomes an idol. Thus, so-called free trade and economic growth have become idols to which the whole world must bow down. Now more than ever, it is critical for U.S. churches, in concert with churches throughout the Americas, to declare, "We will not serve your gods and we will not worship the golden statue that you have set up" (Daniel 3:18).

Unjust trade practices invariably abuse the land and displace workers. Economic injustice deepens as more and more community resources—land and people—are pressed into service of money and of the powerful few who control and trade it. Invariably, this process generates social pyramids in which most of the community's resources are accumulated in the hands of a few, and the community becomes a house divided against itself: of landed and landless, of masters and enslaved, of haves and have-nots.

An Ethic of Marginalized Peoples Confronts an Ethic of Profit Margins

Do not rob the poor because they are poor, or crush the afflicted at the gate; for the Lord pleads their cause.
— Proverbs 22:22–23

For I know how many are your transgressions, and how great are your sins—you who afflict the righteous, who take a bribe, and push aside the needy in the gate. Hate evil and love good, and establish justice in the gate.
— Amos 5:12, 15

In the Bible, "the gate" represents a significant place where communities gather, where the marketplace is located, and where those inside and those outside meet to trade and resolve disputes. It was frequently "outside the gate" where Christians were most active in mission. Paul and Silas met Lydia (a street vendor of purple cloth) outside the gate. It is also where Paul cured a slave girl, which challenged the profit-making interests of those inside the gate (see Acts 16).

In using the image of gates and the division between communities inside and outside the gate to describe the contemporary situation, it is important to stress that there are equally important and divisive gates inside each nation as well as between rich and impoverished nations. Trade agreements, in effect, establish economic and military gates and gatekeepers that regulate trade and movement of goods, resources, and people between those inside the gate and those who are outside, primarily for the benefit of those inside.

From the early 1900s to today, our Church, along with other churches, continues to stand with all who find themselves at the gates and gateways of our globalized society, with workers at factory gates and "free-enterprise zone" gates who face sweatshop working conditions and unlivable wages, at ports with seafarers who move goods for others but have few rights of their own, with migrant workers at national borders between developed nations and developing nations who are judged guilty for where they were born, and with landless farmworkers whose lands have been taken and who now must work for others.

The apostle Paul reminds us that meeting basic needs and sustaining one another's communities is what it means to be members of the same body with gifts "for the common good" (1 Corinthians 12:4–26). The sustainable ordering of society will require participation by all "in order that there may be a fair balance" (2 Corinthians 8:14). This requires U.S. churches to examine our lifestyles and our consumptive and wasteful practices.

Churches face a crucial choice regarding global trade and poverty: *whose side are we on?* Will concern about return on the shares in middle class church endowments and in individual pension funds lead us to align ourselves with corporate interests in profit more than the well-being of people? Or will churches stand for a system of fair trade based on justice and participation by all, especially by marginalized peoples? Our choice will make all the difference.

Notes

1. Thomas Pogge, *Politics as Usual: What Lies Behind the Pro-Poor Rhetoric* (Cambridge: Polity Press, 2010).

2. From an oral presentation at a United Nations briefing on the 1994 United Nations Human Development Report, New York, July 1994.

3. Ben Crow and Suresh K. Lodha, *The Atlas of Global Inequalities* (Berkeley, CA: University of California Press, 2011).

4. See a variety of articles on Bangladeshi workers at International Labor Rights Forum, "Creating a Sweatfree World," www.laborrights.org/creating-a-sweatfree-world.

5. Visit the International Labor Rights Forum homepage at www.laborrights.org.

6. See Environmental Justice Foundation, *White Gold: Uzbekistan, A Slave Nation for Our Cotton?* (London: Environmental Justice Foundation, 2010); Environmental Justice Foundation, *Slave Nation: State-Sponsored Forced Child Labour in Uzbekistan's Cotton Fields* (London: Environmental Justice Foundation, 2009). Both can be accessed at www.ejfoundation.org.

7. International Crisis Group, *The Curse of Cotton: Central Asia's Destructive Monoculture* (New York, International Crisis Group, 2005).

8. Michelle Greenhalgh, "Haitian Farmers Reject Monsanto Donation," *Field Safety News*, June 7, 2010, www.foodsafetynews.com/2010/06/haitian-farmers-burn-monsanto-hybrid-seeds.

9. Beverly Bell, "Haitian Farmers Commit to Burning Monsanto Seeds," May 17, 2010, www.otherworldsarepossible.org/another-haiti-possible/haitian-farmers-commit-burning-monsanto-hybrid-seeds.

10. Anna Lappé, "Who Says Food is a Human Right?" *The Nation*, October 3, 2011.

11. See Michael Nest, *Coltan* (Cambridge: Polity Press, 2011). See also Azadeh Sabour and Matthew Barg, "Complicity in the Congo," Sustainalytics webinar, November 23, 2010, www.sustainalytics.com/conflict-minerals-complicity-congo.

12. For more on the war in Afghanistan and its impact on the people, see David Wildman and Phyllis Bennis, *Ending the War in Afghanistan: A Primer* (Northampton, MA: Olive Branch Press, 2010).

13. "The Economic Community: Poverty," *The Book of Discipline of The United Methodist Church, 2008* (Nashville: Abingdon Press, 2008), ¶163E.

Cheun Keng, a woman in the Cambodian village of Char, works in her rice field. *(Paul Jeffrey)*

Chapter 6

Helping the Global Poor Have a Working Chance

Elizabeth Calvin

- At least 80 percent of humanity lives on less than $10.00 a day.
- More than three billion people—over half the world—live on less than $2.50 a day.
- More than 80 percent of the world's population lives in countries where income differentials are widening.[1]
- Women own just one hundredth of the world's property yet make up the majority of farm labor, sometimes working beside their husbands in the fields or working with other women.[2]
- Women do 66 percent of the world's work and receive only 10 percent of the pay.[3]
- Seventy percent of the world's women live on less than $2.00 a day, compared to 30 percent of men living on less than $2.00 per day.[4]

We are reminded by news coverage every day that we live in a global village. Christians and other people of goodwill believe that with that awareness comes the responsibility of caring for all who live in the village. According to UNICEF, 22,000 children under five years of age die each day due to poverty,[5] and they die quietly in some of the world's poorest villages and communities. There are many forms of aid to the poor (the term *impoverished* more adequately describes the reality): food aid; humanitarian, refugee, and emergency aid; governmental, nongovernmental, faith-based, and private aid; and individual and group charitable aid. Some are efficient, some are inefficient, and some are tied to political and military agendas. This chapter will explore fair trade and microcredit financing, especially for women, as particularly promising ways to ease the tensions of inequality in the distribution of wealth and to alleviate poverty.

Fair Trade

Free Trade is Not the Same as Fair Trade

So what's the difference between "fair trade" and "free trade?" *Free trade* is commonly understood as a system in which goods, capital, and labor flow freely between countries. But the flow is not entirely free. Markets are increasingly being governed by regional and global agreements made between nations. The interests of corporations and powerful nations are shaping world trade and commerce through bodies such as the World Trade Organization (WTO) and in meetings such as the World Economic Forum. One of the criticisms of free trade is that it tends to increase prosperity for a few at the expense of equitable and sustainable development for all. For more than a decade, large demonstrations have been held against the International Monetary Fund (IMF), World Bank, and WTO. The World Social Forum has been the people's counter to the World Economic Forum.[6] United Methodist Women has been an active participant in the World Social Forum, sending teams of staff and directors to the past forums.

Another criticism of free trade is that agreements such as the North America Free Trade Agreement (NAFTA) and the Free Trade Area of Americas (FTAA) are made between partners with unequal negotiating leverage. The agreements reached are between countries with different levels of economic clout, resulting in trade structures that favor wealthier nations to the detriment of poorer countries and impoverished people within those countries.

The Fair Trade Movement

The fair trade movement has grown tremendously in the United States as well as in other countries. Fair Trade USA's motto is that every purchase matters and that fair trade is just that: fair to the farmer or the artisan or the producer of the product in developing countries with just compensation throughout the production process. In this way, fair trade becomes a strategy for poverty alleviation and sustainable development. The goal of Fair Trade USA is to alleviate poverty among farming communities around the world by helping consumers and businesses understand how every purchase matters. The foundational assumption is justice, not charity, and the aim is to alleviate exploitation and promote environmental sustainability.

Historical Streams of the Movement

One stream of the fair trade movement traces its roots to a volunteer for the Mennonite Central Committee (MCC), Edna Ruth Byler, who visited a sewing class in Puerto Rico in 1946 where she found a group of women creating beautiful lace handicraft products while living in poverty. She began to carry their lace pieces back to sell in the United States, returning the money to the women's group. Her efforts grew into what is now known as Ten Thousand Villages, with 2006 sales of more than twenty million dollars within a network of stores all over North America as well as online. Ten Thousand Villages has grown into the largest fair trade retailer in North America because of Byler's thirty-year commitment to the mission of developing fair trade relationships, beginning with selling out of the trunk of her car and evolving into a grassroots movement that became a global network based on the concept and the valuing of fair trade and just relationships.[7]

Another stream of the movement began in 1949 and became known as Sales Exchange for Refugee Rehabilitation and Vocation International, now known as SERRV. SERRV, originally affiliated with the Church of the Brethren, a protestant Christian denomination, has established strong partnerships with Catholic Relief Services and Lutheran World Relief. All items SERRV carries in its product line are fairly traded based on artisan–producer relationships that include respect, transparency, and equity. SERRV works to assist partners in growing their businesses, upgrading skills, improving designs, and finding solutions to their challenges. SERRV is up front in stating support for equal rights for women, sustainable development, and paying a fair wage.

SERRV's fair-trade partners are local organizations such as Fundación Solidaridad, a nonprofit collective of mostly women artisans in Chile. Sara Henriquez, a Chilean woman, began embroidering *arpilleras* with Fundación Solidaridad almost thirty years ago to earn a living during the tyrannical Pinochet dictatorship. Henriquez's designs were protests against the oppression in society at that time, a form of women's resistance art or survival art. *Arpillera* means "burlap" in Spanish. The embroidery is distinctive in its brightly colored patchwork images. Fundación Solidaridad is one of SERRV's partners with a vision of overcoming poverty and providing dignity through work and training. For Henriquez and others, being in a SERRV partner relationship is a form of solidarity that is life changing.[8]

Principles and Benefits of Fair Trade

The Fair Trade Federation, a North American fair trade association, seeks to create greater equity and partnership in the international trading system in the following ways:

- Creating opportunities for economically and socially marginalized producers
- Developing transparent and accountable relationships
- Building capacity
- Promoting fair trade
- Paying promptly and fairly
- Supporting safe and empowering working conditions
- Ensuring the rights of children
- Cultivating environmental stewardship
- Respecting cultural identity

Fair trade practices bring several key benefits:

- They promote gender equality. Women's work is valued and rewarded as much as men's work.
- They help develop small producers independence and improves their management skills.
- They encourage safe and healthy working conditions.
- They encourage business practices that are environmentally sound.

Faith-Based Participation in the Fair Trade Movement

Equal Exchange

Equal Exchange is grounded in an understanding of justice and just relationships based on principles of loving our neighbors, visioning of a better world, accepting that everyone deserves the right to living wages, and insisting that no element of the production chain should be exploitive. A vision of fairness to farmers brought the three founders, Rink Dickinson, Jonathan Rosenthal, and Michael Rozyne, who met in 1986 as managers in a New England food co-op, to conceptualize the new organization called Equal Exchange as an integral part of a movement that is now transforming the relationship between people, the food we eat, and the producers that grow and supply our food. Turning to family and friends for startup funds, the first three years were a struggle until 1994 when strategic funding from the Adrian Dominican Sisters helped other funders and the faith-based community see how this alternative model of doing business with farmers around the world could be successful. In 1996 Lutheran World Relief became a strategic partner in launching what is now known as the Interfaith Program of Equal Exchange. The idea of fair trade was catching on and gaining public acceptance when congregations across the country began using fair trade coffee and teas and, in 2001, fair trade chocolate. Now concerned consumers have an alternative to West African chocolate, which was known to be produced using slavery and child labor. The vision of more equitable relationships with farmers moved from being unrealistic to realistic in a span of twenty years.[9]

Equal Exchange engages in political action to protect the environment, organic consumers, farmers, and cooperatives. This includes advocacy and educating the public about child labor, slavery, and exploitation in the production of some coffee, chocolate, and teas. The first coffee the group chose was called Café Nica, and it was not a coincidence. In 1986, the Reagan Administration had imposed an embargo on products from Nicaragua's Sandinista government. Equal Exchange brought the coffee in through a loophole in the legislation, thereby demonstrating solidarity with the people's movement while challenging what appeared to be an unjust trade policy. Equal Exchange has indeed become the organization that the three visionaries had intended:

> When the new World Day of Prayer USA Committee was formed in 2005, the committee members made a commitment to offering fair trade and women's microcredit products purchased fairly from women's organizations around the world. In this way, women from a wide ecumenical community who are engaged as a part of the World Day of Prayer worshipping community are also intentional fair trade consumers and help to provide support for women's microcredit enterprises in various parts of the world.
>
> (World Day of Prayer USA Committee minutes, 2006–2007)

- A social change organization helping farmers and their families gain more control over their economic futures
- A group educating consumers about trade issues affecting farmers
- A provider of high quality foods that nourish the body and soul
- A company controlled by the people who do the actual work
- A community of dedicated individuals who believe that honesty, respect, and mutual benefit are integral to any worthwhile endeavor[10]

The value, consumption, and awareness of fair-trade consumerism has grown tremendously since the early 2000s and likewise the range of fair trade products has expanded as education and interest in the market has grown. Consumers can easily find fair trade clothing, flowers, coffees, teas, fruits and vegetables, herbs, eco-wines, furniture, and myriad other products. Churches participating in the Equal Exchange Interfaith Program along with The United Methodist Church include the Presbyterian Church USA, the Evangelical Lutheran Church of America, the United Church of Christ, and the Mennonite Church, among others.

Partners for Just Trade

Partners for Just Trade (PJT) began as a nonprofit, faith-based initiative of the Presbyterian Church Hunger Program with the goal of benefitting the participating artisans rather than maximizing profits. The vision was to work with these partners in a fair trade arrangement that would promote social and economic justice and create abundant life for all involved. The artisan groups are encouraged to reinvest profits back into their communities and villages in health clinics, schools, and the like. As a practice, PJT works only with impoverished artisans and groups, defining them as living on less than three dollars per person per day, with some making less than one dollar per day. The artisans and farmers set prices that are fair, that cover the cost of their materials and enable a living wage. PJT has a commitment to address the root causes of poverty through fair trade sales, education, solidarity, and trade justice.[11]

The Blessing Basket Story

The Blessing Basket Project founder Theresa Wilson sees herself as an ordinary person who as a child suffered abuse, resulting in her being taken into state custody. As an adult found herself deserted by her husband and left with two children and little means of support. Acts of kindness and cards of encouragement were given to her by many, and she began to put them in a basket that someone had given to her. The Blessing Basket Project evolved a few years later. She began to speak to women's organizations giving encouragement to overcome obstacles, using a basket holding encouraging notes as a prop. Soon people were asking for the baskets. Knowing what it was like to live in poverty, Theresa set two principles in place as she worked on the model for the basket project: (1) pay the artisan directly without going through a middle person and (2) use the concept of prosperity wage, paying a fair price, thereby elevating the wages of the artisan.

Today, Blessing Basket artisans are paid higher wages than other producers are paid for comparable products, and the financial model is viewed by some as exemplary of "best practices" in poverty reduction. Based in St. Louis, Missouri, several universities are studying the impact of the Blessing Basket Project and its effectiveness in poverty reduction.[12]

Microfinance

The role of the social entrepreneur is to move society from a stable but inherently unjust equilibrium to a new, stable equilibrium that releases potential and alleviates suffering on a major scale. Social entrepreneurs work to ensure that sensible ideas take root and actually change people's thinking and behavior across a society.[13] They initiate, lead change processes, go against the grain, and chart a new path. They are not afraid to experiment, to test the waters, to attack problems, to believe in an idea, to persist when others have doubts, and in many ways are viewed by others as radical. The United Methodist Church and United Methodist Women have long supported microfinancing, sometimes called microlending, microcredit, or microenterprise, as a means of alleviating poverty, especially with women. The terms are often used interchangeably, though some may refer only to lending, while at other times loans and insurance may be included.

What Is Microcredit?

In February 1997, a microcredit summit was held by the Microcredit Summit Campaign in Washington, DC, in which United Methodist Women participated. One outcome was the adoption of a definition for microcredit: "programs extending small loans to very poor people for self-employment projects that generate income, allowing them to care for themselves and their families." The summit also described microcredit in terms of four criteria: (1) size—loans are micro or very small in size, (2) target users—loan receivers are microentrepreneurs and low-income households, (3) utilization—the use of funds are for income generation and enterprise development but also for community use (health, education, etc.), and (4) terms and conditions—most terms and conditions for microcredit loans are flexible and easy to understand and are suited to the local conditions of the community.[14]

Microfinance and Women's Empowerment

Microfinance is generally viewed as a strategy that promotes the alleviation of poverty and as a strategy for women's empowerment in the family and in the community. Individual women or groups of women benefit by having greater access to credit and loans, offered with safe and convenient conditions tailored to the needs of women, thereby increasing income and economic independence. In this way, microfinance is an enabler in expanding the roles of women in the home, in the community, and in society as a whole. Women are enabled to participate in decision making and in improving their status in the home and community. Their contributions to the household often mean that children's school fees can be paid, school uniforms and supplies purchased, and nutrition for the family can be improved. Sometimes this change in the woman's status in the home and community means an altering of traditional roles and the balance of power within the family dynamic, necessitating an adjustment on the part of household members. Overall, women's productive capacities, which may have been neglected previously, are strengthened.

Sou-Sous, a Women's Innovation Out of Necessity

Historically, women have generally had fewer legal rights, banking and credit rights, and less access to banking, credit, and formal savings than men in most societies around the world. Tradition and gender-biased practices that negate the economic and social participation of women brought forth the creativity of women in different ways in order to provide a means for a women's economy. Women long ago achieved status as barterers, craftspeople, and traders traveling across boundaries as needed in order to sell and market their products, to find means of credit, and to accumulate savings outside of traditional systems in which women's participation difficult. The centuries-old West African practice of organizing *sou-sous* has evolved in various forms and can be found not only in West Africa but also in Haiti as *min* and in the Dominican Republic as *sociedad*. Jamaica and Trinidad sometimes refer to it as "partner," while others commonly know the borrowing and saving practice as *sou-sous*. The system gets its name from a Yoruba (Nigerian) term *esusu*, referring to a fund in which several people pool their money. *Sou-sou* may also be derived from a French word *sou*, which means a coin of little value. Typically the participants are close friends, family members, or coworkers who are selected to join an unofficial savings club. It is selective because it is based on the honor system, with no legal paperwork involved, depending only on one's word and one's honor. If a member defaults on a loan, she risks being ostracized in the community, and the *sou-sou*'s organizer generally makes up the amount of the default. Some African and Caribbean immigrants in the United States are in these unofficial savings clubs, each member contributing a specified amount as savings and each member receiving a periodic payout in turn. When that cycle is complete, a new *sou-sou* begins another savings and payout round. *Sou-sous* have been used for mortgage down payments, paying college fees, and paying off debts.

In 2004, Chief Bisi Ogunleye, founder of the Country Women's Association of Nigeria, a past recipient of United Methodist Women's international mission giving, was invited to Trinidad and Tobago in the Caribbean by a group of women to assist those women in understanding the West African *sou-sou* tradition. The aim was to assist low-income women who did not have access to commercial bank accounts to build savings. Chief Bisi had worked for more than twenty years in microfinance and women's banking efforts, establishing one of the first women's banks in Nigeria. The outcome of the meeting in the Caribbean was the Women's Responsive Sou Sou Banking System. The group's stated aims are the following:

- To work with rural and urban low-income women to remove poverty through wealth creation practices and enterprises
- To mobilize, generate, and deliver cooperative community and personal resources for productive and life enhancing ventures
- To promote gender-compliant and women-friendly democratic practices and leadership at all levels of governance[15]

Chief Bisi, as a partner with United Methodist Women, has long believed in the value of wealth creation for women, especially rural women, while also working with urban women. She has proven in her country of Nigeria that microfinance and women's ways of banking, credit, and savings are key to lifting women out of poverty.

A man sells *Real Change*, a newspaper produced and sold by street people in Seattle. *(Paul Jeffrey)*

Adisue Ayu, before she became a Women's World Banking (WWB) client, was a divorced mother of four children with no formal education, living outside of the capital city of Addis Ababa, Ethiopia, with her only possessions being a hut and four sheep. Her first loan was $150 to purchase a cow. The cow produced milk, which Adisue turned into butter and cheese, selling it in the local market. Six years later, she owns five cows, has built a bigger house, all her children are now in school, and she has a monthly salary equivalent to a starting college graduate in Addis Ababa.

(Women's World Banking, "Adisue Ayu: Client of PEACE MFI," www.swwb.org/clients/adisue-ayu-client-peace-mfi)

Examples of Mainstream Microfinance Successes

Grameen Bank, Bangladesh

Not so long ago, it was generally accepted in the world of financial institutions that the poor were high risks for borrowing money, that they would not be able to repay, that rural women in particular were the greatest risk and therefore to be given no consideration for loans, and that the poor could not save money. The Grameen Bank in Bangladesh dispelled these myths and changed the approach to banking with the poor and especially with rural women. They have been providing microloans for thirty-five years. The Grameen Bank and Mohammed Yunus, its founder, received the Nobel Peace Prize in 2006 "for their efforts to create economic and social development from below."[16] Yunus's vision is to harness the power of microcredit to help eliminate poverty in the world.

With women—many of them poor—being half of the world's population, Grameen Bank's approach has shown that women can play a major role in their own economic development and in improving conditions in their homes and communities. Briefly summarized, beginning with small groups of about five members, in lieu of collateral typically required by traditional banks the group is responsible to itself. At first two members apply for a loan, and if their repayment is good, then the next two can apply, and following their repayment, the fifth member can apply. In 1980 there were fewer than 15,000 borrowers. By early 1991, the bank was operating in 854 branches, with more than 900,000 members, of which more than 800,000 were women. In 1992, poor women accounted for 93 percent of the bank's borrowers, and the repayment rate for the bank was 97 percent. What started as an innovative local initiative is now having an impact on poverty alleviation at the national level. Women have been shown to be a better credit risk than men, and the approach is being replicated in countries around the world. By 2006, there were twenty-five Grameen companies providing services in various sectors of society, such as communications, fisheries, Internet service, training and technical assistance, startup funding for entrepreneurs, telecommunications, and health care services, to name only a few. The Village Phone Project with support from one of the companies, Grameen Phone, has helped close to 300,000 women become "telephone ladies" who provide cell phone service to villagers throughout Bangladesh.

The Grameen Bank approach has prompted considerable research, and Yunus has written several books giving more detailed information on the bank. He notes that as microcredit has evolved, so has the understanding of what microcredit means. In his 2007 book *Creating a World Without Poverty: Social Business and the Future of Capitalism,* Yunus categorizes microcredit programs into two clear and distinct types. The first type he calls poverty-focused microcredit programs. Grameen Bank was created to provide this type of program: "poverty-focused," "collateral-free," "low-interest programs." The second type he refers to as profit-maximizing microcredit programs. These programs charge high interest rates, similar to typical profit-driven moneylenders, and therefore cannot be viewed as poverty-focused. Yunus's belief is that microcredit was created to protect the people from moneylenders, not to create more moneylenders.[17]

Women's World Banking

Women's World Banking (WWB), founded in 1976 by Michaela Walsh and several other women and supported in its early days by United Methodist Women, has proven that investing in women can be both profitable as good business and positive in terms of social benefits, having a multiplying effect in the household and community. WWB's vision is that all women will be able to build a secure financial future for themselves and their households. To meet this end, WWB's mission is to help low-income women by helping them access financial services, thereby expanding their economic assets, making them better able to have a decent living and to care for the basic needs of their families. In thirty years, their network has expanded around the world, serving twenty-six million clients, 80 percent of them women, with a savings of $3.5 billion. The WWB global network consists of thirty-nine institutions in twenty-seven countries and includes groups such as Banco da Familia in Brazil, Poverty Eradication and Community Empowerment in Ethiopia, Kenya Women Finance Trust, Microfund for Women in Jordan, Women Development Federation in Sri Lanka, and XacBank in Mongolia. The network members are united in the belief that microfinance must remain committed to providing financial services that meet the needs of women clients. The social impact of serving women is demonstrated and appreciated without compromising the institution's sustainability (see www.swwb.org).

Women's Opportunity Network of Opportunity International

Another successful microfinance organization that has received United Methodist Women's mission-giving support in the past is Women's Opportunity Network (WON), a subsection of Opportunity International. Founded in 1971 as a Christian nonprofit organization by a former president of Bristol Myers and an Australian entrepreneur seeking to transform people's lives without creating dependency, Opportunity International's mission is

---

After becoming a widow, one of WON's education loan clients, Rosemary Namande, of Uganda, started a school for infants in makeshift quarters to support her family while helping others. She started with a group loan of $204. After receiving even larger loans, Rosemary now cares for nine hundred children, fifty-five of whom are orphans and fifteen of whom are HIV positive. She now has five permanent buildings housing an elementary school and orphanage and employs fifty-three people at the school and in her sewing business.

(Opportunity International, "Rosemary Namande," www.opportunity.org/media-center/videos/rosemary-namande/#.TtOzaWDK3Hk)

to bring hope and justice to the poorest of the poor through microfinance. Opportunity International's core values are respect, commitment to the poor, integrity, and stewardship, and are to be demonstrated in their relations with clients, staff, and all people. Along with providing small business loans (starting as small as sixty dollars) and training to people living in poverty in the developing world, Opportunity International now provides innovative programs for insurance protection covering crop damage, unexpected hardships, disasters, and persons infected with HIV and AIDS. Recent innovations in electronic and mobile technology are reducing transaction costs and making services more readily available to people living in remote areas. Opportunity International now has large strategic partners, enabling the organization and its microfinance institutions to expand even more.

In 1991, the Women's Opportunity Network (WON) was formed, providing loans to "trust groups" of ten to thirty entrepreneurs who pledge to guarantee one another's loans. The guarantee of the trust groups eliminates the need for collateral.[18]

United Methodist Women and Youth Support Microfinance
Jam Project in Côte d'Ivoire

In 2001, a United Methodist woman in French-speaking Côte D'Ivoire, Adèle Yed, used $12,400 of her own savings to open a microfinancing bank, Clef Sarepta, to provide loans to help people start or expand businesses. "Clef" means *key* and "Sarepta" refers to Zarephath, the biblical hometown of the widow who was blessed with abundance in the midst of drought because of her trust in Elijah's words (see 1 Kings 17:9). United Methodist Women played a key role in starting the microfinancing program for income-generating activities. In this beautiful country recently beset by political turmoil, poverty is prevalent, unemployment is high, especially among young people, and infant mortality, malnutrition, and malaria are common. United Methodist women's groups in several districts make fruit jam to sell in the churches and markets. The jam provides income for the women and also supports the churches' ministries.[19]

Penny Project at First United Methodist Church, Birmingham, Michigan

The youth group at First United Methodist Church in Birmingham, Michigan, started collecting pennies several years ago, accumulating twenty-three million to represent the number of people infected with HIV and AIDS on the African continent. Beginning the project in 2005 with a general awareness of the devastating spread of the disease, several group members visited Ghana in 2007 to see firsthand how the money would be spent to help children orphaned because of AIDS. Along with support for King Jesus Orphanage, the Penny Project has provided seed money to HIV-infected women to help them start a small income-generating sewing business, and the project has made a large donation to Opportunity International to provide small loans and business training to AIDS victims in Ghana. In addition, the Penny Project has donated scholarship funds for students in the community health program at Africa University in Zimbabwe.[20]

Fonkoze and Lambi Fund: Making a Difference in Haiti Through Microfinance

Fonkoze is an alternative bank for the poor in rural Haiti committed to poverty reduction and serving more than 45,000 women borrowers (mostly living in the countryside) and more than 200,000 savers. Founded by a Haitian Catholic priest, it is built on the recognition that women are the backbone of the economy in Haiti and the caretakers of the family. Fonkoze uses a comprehensive approach of solidarity: group lending, social impact monitoring, small business loans, currency exchange and money transfer/remittances, microinsurance, and postearthquake housing rebuilding and repair services. When the earthquake struck Haiti, Fonkoze lost its headquarters, some employees, and some clients. Since that time, a number of benefactors have stepped forward to assist Fonkoze branches across Haiti, enabling them to become operational as quickly as possible. By far the single largest force of first responders and aid workers has been ordinary Haitian citizens.[21]

Since the earthquake, United Methodist Women have given mission support to Lambi Fund, the Huairou Commission, MADRE, the Movement of Dominican-Haitian Women (MUDHA), the Neges Foundation, and other groups committed to the empowerment of women, particularly women working at the grassroots level of communities, viewing women as equal participants in the rebuilding process in Haiti. A number of vital women leaders in Haiti lost their lives in the earthquake,[22] so strengthening women's leadership is now more important than ever in the rebuilding process. Microfinancing will play a critical role in the way in which women are able to sustain themselves as individuals and groups, taking care of families and communities throughout the countryside. The Lambi Fund's postearthquake work continues with the same philosophy that the fund has always held: providing assistance to peasant-led and women-led community organizations, strengthening the social and economic power of the Haitian people.[23]

Microfinance networks have developed rapidly and grown into regional, national, and multilateral networks and associations for exchanging information and best practices as well as setting guidelines and standards in some institutions. Microfinancing is not the panacea for eliminating or alleviating all of the world's poverty, but it has been shown to have potential for improving the lives of many in the two-thirds world where most of the world's women and children live in impoverished conditions.

Why Should We Care As United Methodist People of Faith?

United Methodist Social Principles call us to be concerned about "the least of these" and to work toward a more just society for all. United Methodist Women's special concern for women and children moves us to become informed and effective advocates of gender equality and the elimination of child labor. Supporting fair trade and microfinance are particular ways we are called to act out our faith.

In the Social Principles ¶163, "The Economic Community" (found in *The Book of Discipline of The United Methodist Church*, 2008), we are called to support measures that would reduce the concentration of wealth in the hands of the few, to advocate for the rights of people to possess property and to earn a living by tilling the soil, and to call on our churches to do all in their power to speak prophetically to the matters of food supply and the people who grow the food for the world. As United Methodists, our church calls us to support fair trade products and its practices of fair wages, equity in relations with artisans and producers, and micro-enterprise in the global south.

United Methodist Resolution 4022, "United Methodist Church Use of Fair Trade Coffee and Other Fair Trade Products" (found in *The Book of Resolutions of the United Methodist Church*, 2008), calls us to use fair trade coffee and other fair trade products. The 2008 resolution also speaks to social purpose lending. The General Board of Pensions has financed nearly $1.5 billion in affordable housing, community health

> Not only is another world possible, she is on her way. On a quiet day, I can hear her breathing.
> — Arundhati Roy

centers, charter schools for low and moderate income people in the United States, and microfinance loans for people in the developing world.[24]

Acting On Our Faith

We are called and we are sent to put our faith into action, to radically love our neighbors as we love our own family. How do we act out our faith in the world today?

1. Through mission giving, United Methodist Women can continue to support the efforts of grassroots women and also the organizations that promote fair trade and microlending to female-led local initiatives.
2. Through the United Methodist Committee on Relief (UMCOR) coffee project with Equal Exchange Interfaith Program, consumers (congregations and individuals) can purchase fair trade coffee, tea, cocoa and chocolate with the assurance that the growers and farmworkers have not been exploited.
3. We can support advocacy networks such as the Huairou Commission and GROOTS International, Rural Coalition, Agricultural Missions, MADRE, Community Food Security Coalition, National Immigrant Farming Initiative, and the National Sustainable Agriculture Coalition. Find and participate in the networks in your local community that are working toward food justice, fair trade, and more just economies and societies.
4. Explore projects like the Blessing Basket to see if your local unit, church, or community can initiate a similar fair trade project.
5. Organizations to explore: Partners for Just Trade, Equal Exchange Interfaith Program, OikoCredit, SERRV International, Foundation for International Community Assistance (FINCA), Aid to Artisans, and Plowshares.
6. Gift-giving seasons are opportune times to express your interest in supporting fair trade and microcredit. Many fair trade retailers have catalogs. If not using catalogs, before selecting gifts, explore fair trade items that can be purchased in your local area. If not already noted on the item, make a card that identifies the item and the producer if you know it. Write a note honoring the artisan and his or her work so that gift recipients are aware they are receiving a fair trade item.

Let us each do our part in ending global poverty by making a commitment to supporting just relationships between artisans, producers, retailers, and shoppers. Fair trade and microfinance are stepping stones out of poverty for many people, especially women in the developing world. We know these women carry the primary responsibility for educating their children, paying school fees, buying uniforms, feeding the family, and taking care of the household in general. By expanding financial services and opportunities for women, their children, families, and communities benefit. Paying a living wage, along with other wealth-creating opportunities, has benefits that multiply in society. The cycles of poverty that go on and on for generations can finally be broken, reducing the opportunity for exploitation of children, youth, women, and the impoverished. In the same way we hope that one day children will ask, "What was war?" we can also hope that in the future, children will ask, "What was poverty and when did we have it?"

Notes

1. Anup Shah, "Poverty Facts and Stats," Global Issues, updated September 20, 2001, www.globalissues.org.

2. Nicole Leistikow, "Women Gain Inch in Push for Land Rights in Uganda," Women eNews, July 20, 2003, www.womensenews.org/story/the-world/030720/women-gain-inch-push-land-rights-uganda.

3. UNICEF, "Gender Equality: The Big Picture," updated August 25, 2004, www.unicef.org/gender/index_bigpicture.html.

4. International Labour Organization, "Facts on Women at Work," www2.ilo.org/public/english/region/eurpro/budapest/download/womenwork.pdf.

5. UNICEF, "Child Mortality Rate Drops by a Third Since 1990," September 16, 2010, www.unicefusa.org/news/releases/child-mortality-rate-drops.html.

6. World Social Forum is an annual meeting of civil society and global justice movement organizations in Porto Alegre, Brazil, with the purpose of offering an alternative future than the one proposed at the annual World Economic Forum held in Davos, Switzerland, with the world's heads of state.

7. Ten Thousand Villages, "Our History: Roots of a Global Movement," www.tenthousandvillages.com/php/about.us/about.history.php.

8. See SERRV, "Artisan Stories," www.serrv.org/category/artisan-stories. Click on "Chile: Fundación Solidaridad, Sara Henriquez" to download a PDF of her story.

9. See Equal Exchange, "Our Co-op," www.equalexchange.coop/our-co-op.

10. Equal Exchange, "Our Story," www.equalexchange.coop/story.

11. Partners for Just Trade, "About Partners for Just Trade," www.partnersforjusttrade.org/ht/d/sp/i/179/pid/179.

12. The Blessing Basket Project, "Founding Story," www.blessingbasket.org/?loc_id=62.

13. Roger L. Martin and Sally Osberg, "Social Entrepreneurship: The Case for Definition," *Stanford Social Innovation Review* (Spring 2007); see also Phil Smith and Eric Thurman, *A Billion Bootstraps—Microcredit, Barefoot Banking and the Business Solution for Ending Poverty* (New York: McGraw Hill, 2007); David Bornstein and Susan Davis, *Social Entrepreneurship: What Everyone Needs to Know* (New York: Oxford University Press, 2010).

14. Language adopted at the original Microcredit Summit Campaign meeting held in Washington, DC, February 2-4, 1997. For more information visit www.microcreditsummit.org.

15. The Network of NGOS of Trinidad and Tobago for the Advancement of Women, "The Women's Responsive Sou Sou Banking System," www.networkngott.org/index.php?option=com_content&view=article&id=12&Itemid=17.

16. "The Nobel Peace Prize 2006: Muhammad Yunus, Grameen Bank," www.nobelprize.org/nobel_prizes/peace/laureates/2006.

17. Muhammad Yunus, *Creating a World Without Poverty* (New York: Public Affairs, 2007). See also Muhammad Yunus, *Banker to the Poor* (New York: Public Affairs, 1999, 2003); Muhammad Yunus, *Building Social Business* (New York: Public Affairs, 2010).

18. Opportunity International, "Women's Opportunity Network," www.opportunity.org/womens-opportunity-network/#.TtOzxWDK3Hk.

19. Tim Tanton, "Fighting Poverty with Jam," United Methodist News Service, July 23, 2009, www.umc.org/site/apps/nlnet/content3.aspx?c=lwL4KnN1LtH&b=5259669&ct=7237963.

20. Joan Kaplan, "Penny Project Uses Pocket Change to Enact Change," United Methodist News Service, December 10, 2008, www.umc.org/site/apps/nlnet/content3.aspx?c=lwL4KnN1LtH&b=2429867&ct=6441973; Mary Jacobs, "Penny Project Nets Big Bucks," United Methodist Reporter, July 18, 2008, www.umportal.org/article.asp?id=3835.

21. See www.fonkoze.org.

22. Tequila Minsky, "A Tribute," **response** 43, no. 5 (May 2011): 31–33.

23. Linda Bloom, "Women Seek Vital Role in Haiti Recovery," General Board of Global Ministries, http://gbgm-umc.org/global_news/full_article.cfm?articleid=5706. See also www.lambifund.org.

24. The General Board of Pension and Health Benefits of the United Methodist Church, "Credit Enhancement and Positive Social Purpose Lending Program," www.gbophb.org/sri_funds/articles/CreditEnhancementPSP.asp.

A boy flies a kite in a camp for homeless families in Jacmel, a town on Haiti's southern coast that was ravaged by the 2010 earthquake. *(Paul Jeffrey)*

Chapter 7

Consumerism and Spiritual Poverty

Paul L. Escamilla

The Name We're Given

"Consumer" is the name we're given by the dominant culture in America. We come by it honestly; the name simply describes, with no effort to euphemize, who we are and what we do. From the first baby blanket to the final burial shroud, from our early morning coffee to our late night social media check-in, whether we're taking in a movie or a milkshake, we are a society that consumes with appetites that are satiated only to be whetted again. "Consumer" is a shoe that fits, and not only do we wear it, we are wondering if it's available in other styles and colors.

Those who selected our name were very careful to shop around before settling on this designation. Other possibilities included "customer," "shopper," "purchaser," "buyer," or, more vaguely, "the market" and "the public." Each of these names had something to commend it, but in terms of possessing the descriptive power to go to the heart of who we are and how we behave, they all paled by comparison with that singularly definitive term, "consumer."

Therefore, when trade journals, government reports, economic assessments, business strategists, or news reporters wish to make reference to our kind, the name they pick, the one to which we readily answer, is that name. It is a name conveniently available in a variety of mix-and-match coordinates, a feature discriminating consumers always appreciate. Among them are consumer affairs, consumer price index, consumer confidence, consumer reports, consumer reviews, consumer action, consumer option, consumer complaints, and, somewhat axiomatic, consumer growth.

Society's frequent use of the term "consumer" turns a lot of attention in our direction, which doesn't appear to bother us. After all, the appellation brings with it certain entitlements (consumer rights), privileges (consumer advocacy), and assurances of fairness in the practice of our craft (consumer protection). It also provides endless social opportunities (consumer groups) or, should we prefer, the option of isolation (consumer privacy). "Consumer" is an equal-opportunity label, making generous accommodations for all sorts of tastes, preferences, lifestyles, and worldviews.

We should understand that refusing to be a consumer altogether is not an option. Rather, consuming is a requirement for survival. We begin to learn this in the womb, the practice field for the consuming life that awaits beyond its borders. At birth our very first act is to purchase a lungful of air at the price of a wail. No sooner have we drawn that breath than we spit and spew and sputter it out before seeking to negotiate another, hopefully at a lesser price. At that breathtaking pace, we move immediately and without apology into milking from our progenitors all manner of goods and services, stopping only to catch our breath again as needed. We nurse at a breast, caress a bottle, fuss for a lullaby; we gum a banana slice, discover birthday cake, down a pizza; we glue ourselves to a screen, shop till we drop, fidget for the latest version of _____ [*you may exercise your consumer option here*]. Our decisions are a constant process of negotiating between wants, wishes, needs, and essentials, and we are often content for others to distinguish, conflate, and confuse these on our behalf. Wants so easily become needs, and wishes, essentials. But even if we're able to maintain a very short list of needs and essentials, we are still utterly dependent on consumption for survival. When it comes to appropriating goods and services, the choice is not whether to be on or off the consumption grid but how deeply enmeshed in that grid we will allow ourselves to become.

Our tenure on this earth would be brutally brief were it not for the nourishment we secure, the shelter we obtain, the clothing we acquire, the fuel that warms the vast majority of us through earth's winters, and the God-given means by which we come by these necessities. Consumption is the required badge at this gala we call life, and regardless of whether we particularly enjoy wearing lanyards around our necks or stickpins on our sweaters, the badge goes with the gala.

Good Eats

In the Bible, consumption is, from the very first, both celebrated and censured, always in that order. Given the tendency to excess that comes with our consuming interest, we might assume that the Bible would bear down heavily on all things material and on human efforts to secure them. What we find, however, is that Scripture treats the subjects of human appetite and acquisition with both remarkable nuance and exemplary restraint.

The book of Genesis opens with a testament to the goodness of a created order within which consumption is a central and sanctioned feature. God's very earliest communication with the human species reads like a pitch from an enthusiastic chef behind the serving line at the cafeteria: "See, I have given you *every* plant yielding seed that is upon the face of all the earth, and *every* tree with seed in its fruit; you shall have them for food" (Genesis 1:29, emphasis mine). The message is not "only one thing is yours" but rather "*everything* is yours." There is a richness and a savor about this inaugural pronouncement that leads the reader to believe that not only is God's world a good world but part of its goodness is the relishing of it. An essential dimension of inhabiting this world is understood to be the appropriation and enjoyment of its provision. (*Provision*, of course, is a word with multiple meanings, a consideration to which we'll return shortly.)

This feast of material goodness is not limited to the human creature either. "And to every beast of the earth, and to every bird of the air, and to everything that creeps on the earth, everything that has the breath of life, I have given every green plant for food" (Genesis 1:30). Following these two extravagant verses—the first referring to humans and the second to other creatures—the narrator adds the validation, "And it was so." It is as if the narrator wanted to address any sense of incredulity on the part of the reader regarding the generosity just recorded on the sacred page. In other words, "Believe it or not, life as the Creator has arranged it to really work that way."

You'll recall the early point of trespass involving the human creatures' failure to observe certain distinctions between that which is *prescribed* for consumption and what, by contrast, is *proscribed* (Genesis 3:1–5). Even in the wake of that moral disaster, God nonetheless furnishes them with clothing (Genesis 3:21). In that moment, and by that remarkable gesture, we become aware that while consumption has its hazards, its radical opposite, complete abstinence, is not a viable alternative. However egregious our gastronomic excesses, we will have to eat again; whatever our infractions against God and one another, we must still be clothed. If with a careless match we've burned our dwelling to the ground, the heat of the blaze searing our face with regret as we look on, the following night is guaranteed to bring with it the need to find some alternative shelter against the cold. Given our own responsibility for putting ourselves in these various predicaments, it is nearly unfathomable that God would be on hand to help us with the task of finding our way out of them. And yet, God is.

The theme of consumption continues in nearly boundless fashion beyond these early Genesis narratives, spilling like a cornucopia onto the pages that follow. Food and drink were the mainstay of conversation between the Israelites and God during their wilderness sojourn, and the Promised Land and its primary description as "a land flowing with milk and honey" became the sought-out destination (see, for example, Deuteronomy 6:3). The Psalms were described by John Donne as "the manna of the church,"[1] and we can see why, for its pages frequently serve up a rich banquet of soul-nourishing metaphors. In Psalm 23, "My cup overflows." Psalm 63 sings, "My soul is satisfied as with a rich feast." From Psalm 145 comes the delighted assurance that "the eyes of all look to you, and you give them their food in due season," and in Psalm 127 your children and mine are regarded as "the fruit of the womb."

Further along in Scripture, prophets insist that chronic hunger has no rightful place among God's children and cast visions in which harvests of plenty are shared by all. Lovers offer themselves to each other as gardens of the choicest fruit, and Jesus dines in both simplicity and splendor, sanctifying these occasions with parables of grace and gestures of forgiveness. The prayer he teaches his first followers is as unapologetic in its wants as an infant at its mother's breast: "Give us . . . forgive us . . . lead us . . . deliver us."

The night before Jesus' arrest and crucifixion, he feeds his disciples once more, instructing them to continue the feast of his life-giving presence and pardon whenever they gather to consume bread and wine. Furthermore, he promises to share the cup with them again in the future reign of God. In three separate resurrection appearances, Jesus eats with his disciples (Luke 24:30 and 41–43; John 21:13). Each of these events affirms the spiritual goodness of material things as well as the human hunger that has its place even on the resurrection side of Easter. In one such appearance, after feeding the disciples, he further cultivates the gastronomic orientation by instructing them, through Peter, to "feed my lambs" (John 21:15–17). Finally, an eschatological vision furnishes us with the view of a New Jerusalem that looks remarkably similar to the original Genesis garden in one particular respect: it makes allowance for physical nourishment. Flowing through the city is a river with a tree along its banks bearing fruit of all kinds, its leaves for the healing of the nations. The vision serves as a reminder of a God whose created order, both original and ultimate, requires and receives sustenance. In other words, we come with an appetite—on purpose. The witness of Scripture is clear: that which is healthy consumes; all that is good, eats.

Provisional Provisions

If the biblical narrative is replete with stories and images validating and even celebrating the human appetite, it also contains a modest counterpoint of censuring that appetite. In other words, its provisions are provisional. Wisdom knows that the membrane between wants and needs is highly permeable, leaving an amorphous and shifting set of indicators by which we distinguish what is enough from what is more than enough. Returning to Genesis, we discover the expansive language of *every*. *Every* is soon qualified by the delimiting designation: *every tree but this one* (Genesis 2:16–17). Scholars and students of the Bible have for centuries explored the question of the precise significance of the tree in question as well as the reasons for the prohibition of its fruit. Through such conversations an entire fund of meanings has grown up, from which I would like to identify one idea that may be helpful to us in the present context.

Drawing primarily on these very same creation texts in Genesis, I suggest that God has a modest aspect, needing little and offering much.[2] Since we are made in God's image, we, too, are fashioned for modesty, for choosing enough over more, adequacy over excess, restraint over extravagance. We have an innate understanding of the difference between "neat," John's Wesley's word for things that were nice enough, and "fine," his description of those things that were, to his way of thinking, a little too nice. In light of this characteristic, could it be that God's provision of bounty, paired with a provision that the couple not eat from a certain tree, is a means of appealing to, even cultivating, their innate capacity for modest choice making? To be mature, both in that original garden and ever since, is to understand how to love but also leave alone. Bounty and boundaries are negotiable realities, kindergarten playmates learning what it means to get along. Give a block, take a block; accept a snack, give some back; state your needs, wait your turn; play well together, find your voice. In kindergarten as in the moral life, harmony depends on how successfully we take into account both self and other, other and self.

In the early decades of the Christian movement, the apostle Paul penned a letter to a church in Corinth that was struggling to weave delight and discipline into a single cloth of common life. His message is both permissive and restrictive: "'All things are lawful,' but not all things are beneficial" (1 Corinthians 10:23). In other words, there are certain things that, while you're free to do them, would not be in either your best interests or those of the community. The capacity for modesty allows for humans to exercise sober and reasonable judgment regarding the fine line between appropriate and inappropriate consumption and so to discover the subsequent sense of fulfillment that always follows such good decisions.

I was in a Jewish synagogue in Portland, Oregon, to lead a workshop some years ago when, during a break, I wandered into the congregation's education wing. In one adult classroom hung a needlepoint rendering of one of our two traditions' most beloved prophetic texts, Micah 6:8. The translation, however, was one I had never seen: "God has told you, O mortal, what is good. And what does the Lord require of you but to do justly, love mercy, and walk *modestly* with your God?" (emphasis mine).

With the change of a single word (from "humbly" to "modestly"), the prophet's meaning was altered ever so slightly, but ever so significantly. Modesty as a framework for casting the vision of the good life for a community of faith strikes me as very close to the Genesis vision of life well lived. It seems abundantly clear from Scripture, as well as our tradition, experience, and reason, that what God requires is generally not radicality but moderation, including matters of what we consume and how we do so. Rather than promulgating an absolute view of choice making, suggesting a precise division between good consumption and bad, we are given a sliding scale, and with it the responsibility to engage our conscience and its divinely endowed sense of modesty. We are, in other words, given the freedom to enjoy earth's provisions provisionally.

Lather, Rinse, Repeat

"The marketplace" is a reference to those of us who at any given time wish to interest others in our brand or version of things. The tendency of the marketplace has always been to capitalize on the human propensity to drift from modest to more, removing the "provisional" from "provisions." The historical privilege and predicament of recent generations of many Americans, however, is that "more" has been more accessible than ever before. For virtually all societies preceding our own, plenty was reserved for the few and excess for the fewer. Royal treatment was, well, *royal* treatment, restricted to the elite upper margins of society. The vast majority of individuals within a given community or nation-state lived either adequately or hand-to-mouth. Over the past half century, however, Western economies of scale have provided unprecedented access to excess. In such societies, more people than ever before can be overfed, overclothed, overfurnished, and overburdened.

Some historical context may be helpful here. In the 1950s a concerted effort was made in this country to accelerate both production and consumption. The increased capacities of postwar producers to manufacture goods, combined with the newly augmented spending power of the American public, made the idea of ramping up both supply and demand not only attractive but entirely feasible. Since manufacturers had more than enough product-generating capacity to satisfy consumer needs at existing levels, consumers were, more than ever before, and in increasingly sophisticated ways, invited to purchase and consume beyond their reasonable needs. Economist Victor Lebow, in what has proved to be a prescient article published in 1955, sized up this strategic marketing approach quite transparently: "Our enormously productive economy demands that we make consumption our way of life, that we convert the buying and use of goods into rituals, that we seek our spiritual satisfactions, our ego satisfactions, in consumption . . . We need things consumed, burned up, worn out, replaced and discarded at an ever-accelerating pace."[3]

The approach took hold, and over time a marketing apparatus emerged with the goal of creating perceptions of need where no real need existed. In Edenic terms, the serpent was on point, persuading the couple, with the rest of us within earshot, that they needed more than what they truly needed. A simple example of how such a strategy has played out in advertising and product promotion is as close at hand as a shampoo bottle. Its instructions have become a household phrase: Lather, rinse, *repeat*. Where once *a* shampoo of our hair would have been a shampoo, we have been groomed to understand shampooing our hair to involve multiple applications of the product. If one application of shampoo is adequate, a second must be even better. The reasoning becomes comically circular if the instructions on the bottle are followed literally: lather, then rinse, then repeat: lather, then rinse, then repeat: lather, then rinse, then. . . .

We may find the idea more amusing than worrisome. After all, we're way too smart to allow anyone to dupe us into shampooing our hair ad infinitum, purchasing more and more of a product for that purpose. And yet, in a sense, that is precisely what we routinely do. It may be conditioner that is the follow-up step, or hair color, or a trim, a treatment, straightening, curling, volumizing, and so on. It may be a larger container of shampoo at the same price, or two for the price of one, or a nicer brand than we've used in the past. In one way or another, we often find ourselves walking that comic circle in spite of ourselves. Some time ago I entered a convenience store for the express purpose of buying a single banana. I left the store with two bananas, a shift that can be explained by a simple line spoken by the cashier: "They're two for a dollar."

"Lather, rinse, repeat" has many permutations, but all have in common the subtle or not-so-subtle insinuation that once is never enough, more is always better, and there is always something else needed in order to complete the cycle of incompleteness. As it has been said, for Americans, a good thing is okay, more of a good thing is better, and too much of a good thing is just about right.

Our Consuming Interest

What are the liabilities of such a way of practicing consumption—or overconsumption—as individuals and a society? To begin with, our planet is taxed by increased production on the one hand, overuse on the other, and waste resulting from both. When both producers and consumers narrow their focus to the product being traded, attention is turned away from any wide-reaching effects of that transaction. Collateral issues regarding limited natural resources, landfill challenges, and other pollution burdens are ignored, and we all suffer. In addition, goods and services when enjoyed to excess by one population become unavailable to others in even basic ways. A modern message that speaks with utter clarity to this particular concern is "Live simply, that others may simply live."

Living by patterns of excess creates one further hazard intrinsically related to these first two: spiritual poverty. Selling for the sake of selling and buying for the sake of buying swiftly become soulless enterprises that leave both buyer and seller bereft of any sense of moral or spiritual identity or direction. When the focus of our attention and resources is shampoo or bananas, entertainment or acquisitions, our capacity to be attentive to God, others, creation, and our own deepest needs and aspirations in relation to these is significantly diminished.

In this regard, the dual function of "consume" should not escape our notice. The word, drawn from the Latin *sumere*, "to take," toggles between active and passive voice in a way that is far too close for comfort. Consumption is, ostensibly, what we take in the way of other objects (e.g., shampoo, the latest movie, a banana or two). However, in a more subtle way, consumption is also what is taken from us. "A consuming interest" is not simply a reference to what we enjoy; it also describes what occupies us, makes a claim on us, *consumes* us. If our particular consuming interest is the excessive acquisition of things, experiences, and the like, then sooner or later we will be nibbled to nothing by the practice of it.

In centuries past, "died of consumption" was a common reference to a certain illness having taken its ultimate toll. The name of this disease has since been refined to something more clinically descriptive—tuberculosis—leaving the former label available for other purposes. "Died of consumption" can now be used to describe any of an array of causes for a person's spiritual demise, all having to do with failing to distinguish between modest and excessive, neat and fine, enough and too much.

The Gospels relate to us that Jesus was once approached by someone very much like you and me (Mark 10:17–22). This person is both good and well provided for; he is a man of means and morals, we might say. He wants

A girl left homeless by fighting between the forces of rebel Tutsi General Laurent Nkunda and the Congolese government carries water in a displaced persons camp in the village of Sasha, in eastern Congo. *(Paul Jeffrey)*

to know God, love God, and follow God, and believes Jesus may help him find the best ways to do so. They review the teachings together, the traditional commandments, and the man confirms that he has observed these from his youth. He is a good churchgoer, a law-abiding citizen, a decent person. We're told that at this point Jesus looks at the man with love in his eyes. Maybe he does so because he knows that what he is about to ask of the man will challenge him to the core of his being, or maybe because he knows that what he is about to ask of him will enable him to experience life in more profoundly meaningful ways than he has ever dreamed possible. We're not told why Jesus looks at him with love. We can only suppose it is for a similar set of reasons that he looks at us the same way. And he says to this man who is both good and well provided for: "Go, sell what you own, and give the money to the poor, and you will have treasure in heaven; then come, follow me."

We often understand this encounter to be about personal discipleship, *my* own journey of faith. I wonder if instead it might be about *shared* discipleship, about choosing to relate to both the world and Jesus at a new and deeper level, for the sake of all involved. The final subject of the conversation, after all, is the basic needs of others. The seeker's willingness to address these needs is the key to discovering spiritual treasure for himself. "Pity is the password," the novelist Vladimir Nabokov once suggested.[4] By pity he surely meant not merely an ability to sympathize but an action resulting from that feeling.

The person in the story responds in shock to Jesus' directive and goes away grieving, for, as we have said, he is both good and well provided for, a combination guaranteed to stir up moral and spiritual quandaries every time. We've often assumed his emotional reaction signifies a "no" to the plan Jesus has just suggested. The man is in grief over having to walk away from such a promising and profoundly meaningful way of life due to the powerful claim his consumables make on his very being. But I like to imagine a different scenario: the man is in grief as he does the mental inventory of all those things he so treasures—furnishings, keepsakes, landscapes, clothes, collectibles, concert tickets, power tools, a well-stocked kitchen, favorite books. You know the list; it's your list, too. He has, beyond his initial shock, decided for that promising and profoundly meaningful way of life. Every step he now takes in the direction of home brings him closer to relinquishing his consuming interests, an action he both dreads and determines he will undertake for the sake of being in relationship with the poor and with the teacher from Galilee. Jesus has clearly connected both relationships with spiritual wealth and redemption. "Share . . . and follow," Jesus has said to the man of means and morals as if they were in some sense one and the same. Perhaps they are.

Reverse Miracles

As the dust settles behind the seeker who is now heading for home to make the decision of his life, Jesus warns his disciples that it is harder for those who are rich to enter the reign of God than for a camel to pass through the eye of a needle (Mark 10:23–25). We often understand this warning to suggest that the rich—a term that surely includes the majority of those of us living in the United States—are encumbered by many things and are therefore unable to pass along a narrower, more spiritually inviting way. The maintenance and management of our possessions and pursuits leaves the reservoir of our souls drained dry. Either way, we are left so consumed by what we consume that our fancy water buckets turn out to have holes in the bottom.

Lately I've begun to consider one further possibility. Perhaps what makes it most difficult for us who are rich to participate in the reign of God is this: while sharing with others is the means by which we find the path that leads to Jesus and eternal life, overconsumption is essentially a solitary act. As a robust consumer, I accrue, aggregate, and acquire, placing myself at the center of that enterprise. The reign of God, by contrast, is an invitation to a communal feast in which life's bread is taken, blessed, broken, and *shared*. Instead of the host at the head of my own dinner table, I become a guest at another's—a change of seats that poses the risk of losing far more than proximity to my favorite casserole.

When Jesus looks at a wealthy seeker with love in his eyes, it must be in part because he understands the myriad complicating forces involved in that shift from loving things to loving people and from indulging self to ennobling self through serving and empowering others. Though we have been created to know in our hearts what truly matters in life and to seek after these things, sin has left us an addled race, "mistaking value for the price," as songwriter Paul Simon has recently put it. We often confuse our truest longings with more shallow wants and appetites, leading us to try to satisfy deep yearnings by superficial means. As a cartoon has quipped, "When I'm trying to make a decision, I always listen to my gut; it usually tells me to eat chocolate."[5]

Even when we know what's right, healthy, healing, and responsible—and what, by contrast, has been hurtful or diminishing—we sometimes seem oblivious to having made poor choices in the past or helpless to make better ones in the future. When a group of tourists visiting an Amish community was asked by their guide how many of them felt they would be better off if they did not own a television, nearly every hand went up. When the guide then asked how many in the group, upon returning home, would discard their television sets, all raised hands quietly returned to their laps.

In response to Jesus' assertion that it is difficult for the rich to participate in God's new society, the disciples ask, "Then who can be saved?" Jesus answers, "For mortals it is impossible, but not for God; for God all things are possible" (Mark 10:26–27). We who face the predicament of being overtaken by our excessive practices of taking will need a divine miracle to be lifted and enlightened into living another way. In this dialogue between Jesus and the disciples, we must count on his final words to be the *first* words of God's mercy and renewing power in our lives: "For God all things are possible."

An ancient legend tells of a man who wished for a place where he could take in life's pleasures unencumbered by all the burdens others placed on him. One day his wanderlust led him from his village in search of his imagined Paradise. Every night as he pitched his tent by the roadside, he would remove his shoes and point them in the direction he was headed so as to be certain of his course when he resumed his journey the following morning. One night as he slept an angel came and turned his shoes in the opposite direction. The following morning, the man awoke, put on his shoes, and continued his journey. After some days he arrived at a small village that seemed strangely familiar and equally alluring. He turned down a street that left him marveling at its ordinary appeal. He entered a house he faintly recognized, a rather unremarkable structure that he couldn't help but find beautiful without being able to say why. At the door he was greeted by a family whose eager faces elicited a sudden recollection, warming his heart beyond measure. As he embraced his loved ones, he thought to himself, "What a miracle! I have surely found my way to Paradise."

"The angels keep their ancient places," the poet assures us,[6] and they work their reverse miracle along all the myriad trails that carry humans toward their misdirected aspirations. "For God all things are possible," including turning our steps in the opposite direction, opening our eyes to true beauty and our hearts to true understanding. It turns out we still know, deep within, the difference between what we think we want and what we truly need. Deep within, we realize that the good life has very little to do with strapping ourselves to more and more creature comforts and very much to do with accepting the invitation to share life's sacred journey with God, one another, and all creation.

Our Given Name

If the name we're given to describe who we are and what we do is "consumer," there's another name that describes who we *truly* are and what we are *created* to do. That word is "companion." It is a gift from the Latin, and in that tongue the word means "with bread" but is just as easily rendered "bread with." Either direction, a companion is one with whom bread is shared. I like to believe if "consumer" is the name we're given, then "companion" is our given name. At baptism we are washed in water from another's well, offered to God by many hands, prayed over with borrowed words, and drawn up from the font only to be given over into others' care. In this sacramental act God's name is spoken quite near our own, and our own name in turn very near that of the community, rendering us all companions for life.

The Eucharist, in a way that is both self-evident and shrouded in mystery, also regards us as companions. The four-action shape of Jesus' final meal with his disciples was mentioned previously: Jesus took bread, blessed it, broke it, and shared it with the disciples. We enact that very same sharing at the Lord's table, calling the holy meal "communion" because of our "common union," or shared union, with Christ, one another, and the world.

The bread and wine of the Eucharist recall the community garden of Genesis, in which God created all things good and provided the wherewithal for humans to practice companionship and care as the means to experiencing well-being and abundance. As these companions shared the tending work and bountiful yield of the good earth, they were meant to discover deep fulfillment in their self-giving, a disposition reflecting God's own nature. It was, after all, the primordial gift of divine breath that first awakened these clay forms, God's self-giving for the life of the world. Made in God's image, it is our nature, too, to spend our days, our years, our lifetimes breathing life into the world around us. We tend the world's gardens of promise and of need, giving what we possess to those within our ever-widening reach of care. As we do so, we discover deeper strength and generosity to give again and yet again, and we find increasingly greater joy in the giving. For beneath all the give and take of tending life's many gardens is the mystery of God's grace blessing us with precisely that which we have given away and thereby making of us more than what we ever hoped to be.

In the central paradox of living by faith, receiving is understood as merely a channel for giving and giving as the means by which we come to know life in abundance. Companions are those who share their bread, and so are fed. Our various gifts and graces are briefly housed within our frame as though we were a way station on the path leading from God to others. The peasants of Haiti have blessed us with a proverb that expresses this reality beautifully: *Bondye konn bay, men li pa konn separe.* "God gives but doesn't share." God gives people what they need, but sharing, the original burden-blessing of companionship, is left to us.[7] Creation, font, table, Scripture, and life lived in community and creation all bid us to turn from God toward one another with a disposition of needing little and offering much. We not only bring God with us when we turn in such a way, we meet God there as well, in the world to which we go, in those with whom we share. "As you did it to one of the least of these . . . you did it to me" (Matthew 25:40).

"Companion" is a given name both too big for us and perfectly suited. We glimpse something of ourselves in the name, then live on to participate in the miracle of becoming, by God's grace, more like what we've glimpsed. Day by day, gesture by gesture, deed by deed, we are more and more companions with one another, expressing our thanks for all that has been given us by making those gifts an offering. With every decision to surrender rather than grasp, bestow instead of hoard, and trust beyond our fear, we are nourished on the bread that is first taken, as all bread must be, and then blessed, broken, and shared.

Notes

1. From a sermon on Psalm 63:7 preached at St. Paul's Cathedral, London, January 29, 1625.

2. See my earlier development of this idea in Paul Escamilla, *Longing for Enough in a Culture of More* (Nashville: Abingdon Press, 2007), 10–11.

3. Victor Lebow, "Price Competition in 1955," *Journal of Retailing* (Spring 1955).

4. Vladmir Nabakov, *Pale Fire* (New York: Lancer Books, 1989), 225.

5. Quote seen on a memo pad in a gift store.

6. Francis Thompson, "The Kingdom of God," in *The Oxford Book of English and Mystical Verse*, eds. D. H. S. Nicholson and A. H. E. Lee (Oxford: Clarendon Press, 1917).

7. See Tracy Kidder's book about Dr. Paul Farmer, *Mountains Beyond Mountains* (New York: Random House, 2003), 79.

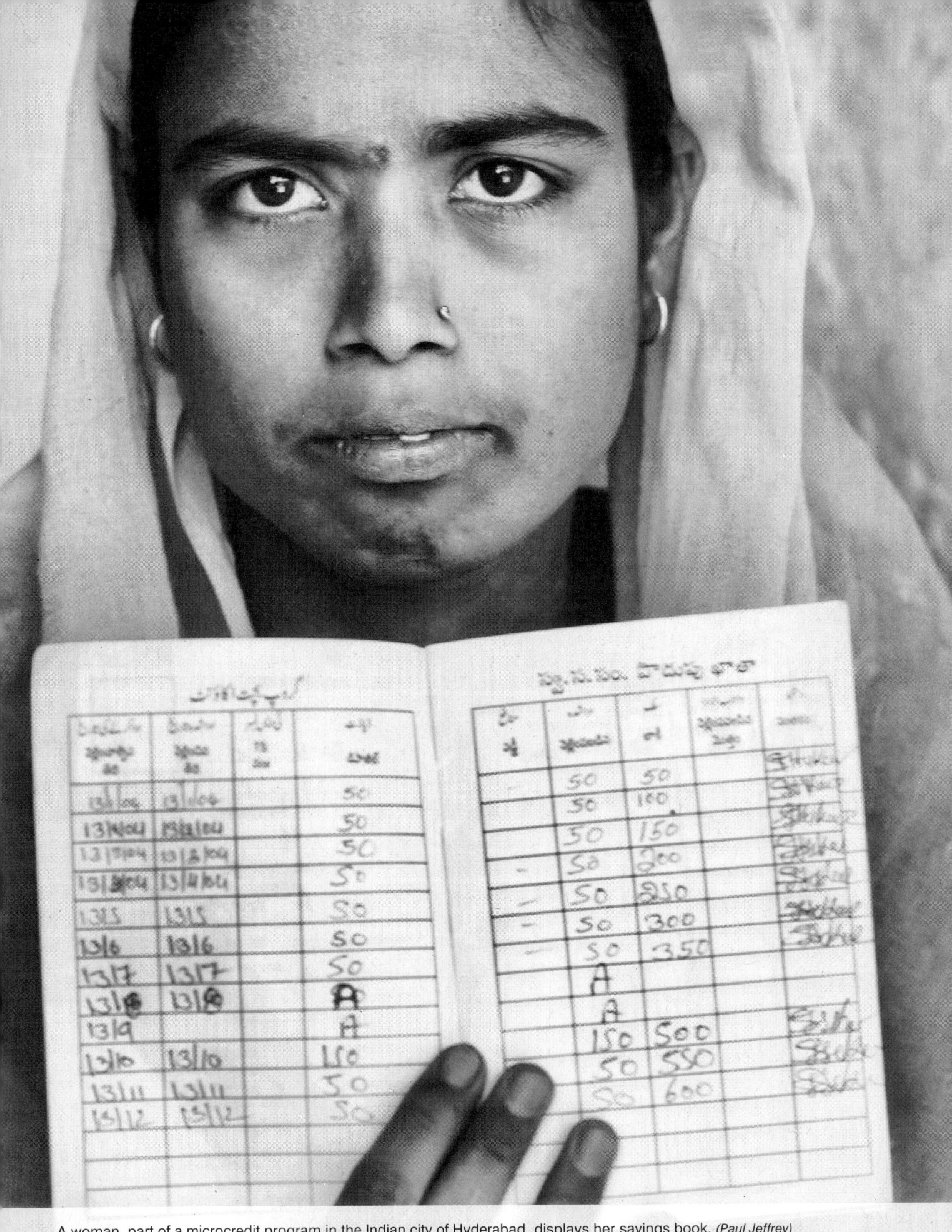

A woman, part of a microcredit program in the Indian city of Hyderabad, displays her savings book. *(Paul Jeffrey)*

Chapter 8

Charity Is Not Enough

Sung-ok Lee

> Poverty most often has systemic causes, and therefore we do not hold poor people morally responsible for their economic state.
>
> — From the Social Principles of The United Methodist Church, *The Book of Discipline of The United Methodist Church*, ¶163E.

What Is the Difference between Charity and Justice?

Charity is associated with acts of kindness. There are times when charity can be an appropriate and necessary response to people in crisis. It can be a lifeline to people on the verge of drowning. However, there are limitations associated with the giving of charity, limitations that challenge us to move beyond charity to *justice*. So why isn't charity enough? Bishop Peggy Johnson, United Methodist episcopal leader of the Eastern Pennsylvania Conference, lays out several valid points about the limitations of charity:

- With charity, the life of the receiver does not change for the long term. Charity gives a momentary reprieve, but it does not provide a lasting solution to the problems of life.
- Charity is seductive. It makes the giver feel good about helping someone in need. This "high" can actually help preserve the unjust system that makes the giving of charity necessary.
- Charity can also cause shame. This results as receivers find themselves in a vulnerable situation, dependent on others for help.
- Charity can lead to fatigue in the giver. After responding a few times with help, people are often eager to help someone else. This is why food closets often have a limit to how much and how often they will help one individual. When the allotted services have been used up, the person in need has to go without.
- With charity, the giver feels good, relieved of guilt, but the recipient soon feels the same old hunger pains. In fact, the giving of charity can actually make a bad situation worse as the root cause continues to exist but the motivation to solve the problem is alleviated.[1]

Chapter 1 of this book asks the question, "Are we avoiding or encountering the poor?" This chapter asks a parallel question: Are we avoiding or encountering the root causes of poverty?

Much of the world's population is denied access to opportunities and resources due to conditions of poverty. When we look at the root causes underneath the symptoms of poverty, we find structures that keep people in poverty. Unfair systems cause and perpetuate the vicious cycle of poverty. But there can be healing, and it takes more than prayer; it takes awareness, advocacy, and hard work to dismantle these unjust systems.

This work begins with an analysis of power. We need to understand how systems work in order to challenge them. In a world of God's abundance, people are poor not because of their own deficiencies but because others have amassed great wealth. This happens between individuals, within nations, and between nations. This is possible through unequal power, often imposed by force. In many cases, such power is a reflection of race, gender, class, age, nationality, ethnicity, or other privileged status. So we must ask some questions to help us understand systemic injustice that is at the root of poverty: "Who owns? Who decides? Who wins? Who loses? What is the historic and current context that created this situation? What action can directly address power imbalances to change this picture?"[2]

United Methodist Women Engages in Poverty Survey

In pursuing the encountering of the root causes of poverty, United Methodist Women's national board of directors recommended in fall 2001 that a poverty survey be conducted across the country with the help of the social action officers at the annual conference level as well as at the local level. After much planning and consulting, the section on Christian Social Responsibility of United Methodist Women's national staff office conducted a poverty survey in summer 2004, implemented by social action mission coordinators from local United Methodist Women units. The survey was a means of helping members of local units gather some basic data about the economic and social conditions in their communities. This data was collected and analyzed and was used to support United Methodist Women in discerning and addressing the issues of poverty.

Diane Dujon and Ann Withorn with the University of Massachusetts worked on a comprehensive data analysis of the surveys[3] completed by the social action mission coordinators. The results indicated that United Methodist Women members gained critically important knowledge about how poverty was affecting their communities and society in general.

Members reported, "Most of this experience, our first, has broadened our knowledge of what it means to be poor as well as knowing about the social services and community supports available in our community. We've been blessed." "Thank you for showing how big the problem is." All of the survey respondents checked the following as economic concerns for their communities:

- Unavailable and/or inadequate affordable housing
- Lack of access to health care for adults
- Low wage jobs
- Lack of employment opportunities

More than half of the surveys also noted the importance in perpetuating poverty of such issues as the following:

- Lack of transportation
- Lack of good child care
- Not always enough money for food—especially for homebound elders and the disabled
- Mental health and substance abuse issues
- Domestic violence
- Immigration-related issues (status and language)
- HIV/AIDS
- Poor neighborhood conditions creating isolation and fear

Most surveys reported that their church members were engaged in at least two poverty-related activities, such as:

- Food pantries and food delivery to seniors/disabled people
- Food kitchens and meals on wheels
- Clothing and furniture relief collection
- Volunteer programs in emergency shelters
- Tutoring programs and school lunch support
- Summer camps for indigent children
- Special collections for local and international charities
- Home visits to different types of elderly and disabled people

Dujon and Withorn recommended that additional sources of knowledge be made available to local congregations. They noted that one of the most telling revelations from the survey was how much United Methodist Women members still have to learn about social services and avenues of advocacy that are available to help alleviate poverty. Members learned that antipoverty work was never only the responsibility of state bureaucracies. Antipoverty work was not only the task of soup kitchens, day care providers, and health care centers. They learned that knowing about local employment options helps, but so does knowing what the rules are in one's state for supplemental security income (SSI), unemployment benefits, workers' compensation, and access to Temporary Assistance for Needy Families (TANF) programs and what is available as backup for those who depend on part-time employment and occasional employment for survival. They learned that "welfare," SSI, Medicaid, and other programs existed that could be built back up and improved. But this would not happen if people thought every social obligation had devolved back "to the community" and was now left totally up to nonprofits, as some of the survey respondents assumed.

Dujon and Withorn also advised United Methodist Women to obtain further information about what remained of the "economic safety net" where members' congregations were located. They suggested that members do the following:
1. Find out if there was still a real base for economic rights, benefits, and services, contrary to what some seemed to think.
2. Consider seriously what it would take for a person or family to get benefits or to be ineligible for them (many respondents either vastly under- or overestimated this).
3. Become both more knowledgeable and more humble when talking with low-income people, allies, and advocates regarding how people manage with so little.

They recommended further that United Methodist Women's future work focus on poverty among families struggling to maintain hope for their children's future and engage with those families as allies in change efforts, not as "others" whose problems deserve charitable service at best.

Finally, the consultants urged members not to forget that we are a faith community. We are a faith-based organization with political influence on welfare reform. The history of our particular church includes a deep vein of the Social Gospel, of bringing our beliefs and values into the world in a holistic way.

Dujon and Withon are the editors of *For Crying Out Loud: Women's Poverty in the United States*.[4] In the book they make the following points regarding women and poverty:
- The problems that women on welfare face are connected to the dilemmas that low-income workers encounter, and the troubles low-income workers experience are not that different from those confronting more "middle-class" workers.
- The identification with low-income women is not a simple one, and solutions to women's poverty must be varied due to the differences in cultural backgrounds of women themselves, even as the struggle for economic and political power for all must be joined. The failure of the welfare system, which no one knows better than poor women, should lead to calls for a better, more fully accountable welfare state, not to demands for less government.
- Women can speak for themselves, regardless of their situation.
- The problems facing poor women, facing all women, facing everyone, are political in their solutions,

no matter how deeply economic, structural, gendered, moral, or cultural their cause.
- "Crying out loud," banding together, organizing, strategizing, and educating ourselves together can make a difference.

Pursuing Justice: Linking Service and Advocacy

So how can justice be lived out in our daily lives as we walk with and work with the poor? Much has been done by United Methodist Women and others in The United Methodist Church in pursuing the eradication of poverty. From the Bishops' Initiative on Children and Poverty to the Ministry with the Poor Task Force, our church has been at work to alleviate the suffering of the most vulnerable of our society.

For the rest of this chapter, I want to illustrate how we have taken on the challenge posed by Dujon and Withorn through our recent history to the current time to continue to "cry out loud," band together, organize, strategize, and educate ourselves together to make a difference for women and children.

Thousands of members of United Methodist Women have written letters to presidents on behalf of women, children, and families regarding issues that affect their very survival, and they have stood in public witness and silent vigils for fairness and rights for their welfare. In fall 1990 we sent letters with a delegation of officers to the White House to express to President George H. W. Bush our concern regarding (1) the lack of action by the administration in support of families and children and (2) the vetoes of the Family and Medical Leave Act and the threatened vetoes of the Civil Rights Restoration Act and child care legislation. We supported and partnered with state projects of Interfaith IMPACT for Justice and Peace, an interfaith organization of denominations and faith groups, local and regional affiliates, and people of faith seeking to advance the cause of justice, peace, and stewardship of creation in the public policy arena. Our members worked with the Florida IMPACT Community Childhood Hunger Identification Project, a statewide interfaith legislative action network that focused on issues of hunger, affordable housing, and equity for farmworkers. IMPACT helped keep member groups informed on issues of social and economic justice as they became matters of public policy through workshops, regular publications, media events, and phone tree activity. The project's initial goal was to be able to form Florida's Statewide Homeless Coalition, creating and sustaining funds for the state emergency homeless assistance program for families and securing a state mandate for school breakfast programs after a ten-year effort. Once the project's education phase was over, the goal became the establishment in Polk County of a self-sustaining, self-governing, community-based organization of low-income women that would continue to address the immediate needs of low-income families while maintaining a voice in public policy.

In the 1990s, United Methodist Women supported a national letter-writing campaign to eliminate sweatshops by sending letters to retailers, manufacturers, and product endorsers and then circulating those letters to United Methodist Women conference leaders. We partnered with grassroots group La Mujer Obrera of El Paso, Texas, which represents the concerns of women in their community who face health and safety problems, low wages with no benefits, and the threat of harassment if they try to organize. This work continues today with our partner National Mobilization Against Sweatshops in addressing injured workers fighting for the right to compensation and medical benefits and supporting garment, restaurant, construc-

The Gateway Arch in St Louis, Missouri, as seen from a dump—part of the urban landscape in East St. Louis, Illinois. *(Paul Jeffrey)*

tion, and office workers—many of whom are people of color and immigrants—in standing up against long work hours and hazardous working conditions.

Boycotts, only as approved by the General Conference of The United Methodist Church, have also been a way to fight poverty. United Methodist Women has a long-standing partnership with the National Farm Worker Ministry (NFWM), participating in boycotts of grapes, strawberries, Campbell's Soup, Taco Bell, and Mt. Olive Pickle to support fair wages and decent working conditions for farmworkers. NFWM is an interfaith organization that supports farmworkers as they organize for empowerment, justice, and equality. It began in 1920 as a ministry of charity and service, providing food, clothing, and day care to farmworkers. When United Farm Workers founder Cesar Chavez began organizing in the 1960s, he called on the religious community to change its emphasis from *charity* to *justice*. NFWM became the vehicle for people of faith to respond to that call. NFWM brought together national denominations, state councils of churches, religious orders and congregations, and concerned individuals to act with farmworkers to achieve fundamental change in their living and working conditions. Grounded in faith, we joined NFWM to work side by side with farmworkers throughout the country, organizing vigils, picketing, coordinating boycotts, and educating constituents. We continue to engage in this ministry of advocacy as an integral part of the NFWM.

Also living out a ministry of service and advocacy, United Methodist Women joined the Coalition for Justice in the Maquiladoras and endorsed the standards of conduct as defined by the coalition and participated in shareholder actions calling for companies operating *maquiladoras* to comply with environmental regulations, worker safety and health regulations, fundamental worker rights, and community infrastructure needs.

The Campaign for Children: Improving Children's Lives

In the late 1980s it became very clear that fighting poverty involved improving the lives of children. In 1998, United Methodist Women began a five-year Campaign for Children. In April 1990 at its national assembly United Methodist Women collected ten thousand signed postcards urging President George H. W. Bush to sign into law the child care legislation passed by the House of Representatives and the Senate earlier that year to meet the needs for safe, quality, affordable child care. We also urged the president to support the United Nations Convention on the Rights of the Child. The president signed into law the Child Care and Development Block Grant Act in 1990.

The Campaign for Children called on each of the nearly thirty thousand United Methodist Women local units to study the status of children in their local municipalities, counties, and states and to take action through community service and political advocacy. The campaign urged members to involve their entire congregations in their activities and to join with other community groups and churches for public awareness and action on behalf of our nation's children. In the first two years of the campaign, more than 2,500 local units formally joined the campaign as active participants.

During phase II of the Campaign for Children (1994–1999), women stood outside the White House with signs that said, "Making the World Safe for Children and Youth in the 21st Century," and they called for the following:

- Funding for expansion of Head Start Programs and the Special Supplemental Food Program for Women, Infants, and Children (WIC)
- Comprehensive health coverage for all Americans, especially pregnant women and children
- National child support legislation and additional legislation designed to assure education and training opportunities for welfare recipients and the availability of quality child care for children of low income parents participating in education or training or at work
- Changes in the law to ensure that a person working full time at the lowest wage level can earn an income above the poverty level and support her or his family, such as supporting increases in the minimum wage and further expansion of the earned income tax credit

Implementation of phase II of the Children's Campaign was shared by the following four United Methodist Women conference mission coordinators: supportive community, Christian personhood, global concerns, and Christian social involvement. The Women's Division of the General Board of Global Ministries of The United Methodist Church, the national policymaking body of United Methodist Women, also encouraged conferences, districts, and local units to promote actively the programs of the United Nations Children's Fund (UNICEF). United Methodist Women's Office of Children, Youth, and Family Advocacy worked with RUGMARK,[5] an organization dedicated to ending child labor in the rug-making industry, for a comprehensive consumer education campaign, printing ten thousand grassroots action kits, which were twelve-page booklets to be distributed to a broad coalition of organizations working against child labor and for fair trade.

In fall 2006, the United Methodist Women board of directors voted to support the State Child Health Program (SCHIP) being taken to Congress and joined many partners working to push this legislation. The directors invited members of local units to sign petitions and send them to Washington so Congress would know their concern about the millions of uninsured children in our nation. The legislation passed Congress but was vetoed by President George W. Bush. An action alert was sent in early 2007 to ask members of United Methodist Women to keep putting pressure on their representatives.

On February 4, 2009, President Barack Obama signed the State Children's Health Insurance Program (SCHIP) Reauthorization of 2009. It provides insurance for an additional four million children and eliminates some of the barriers to getting benefits.

The SCHIP Reauthorization is a good step forward, but there is still work to be done. An additional five million or more children are still without health coverage today, along with some forty-six million Americans overall.[6] Affordable and accessible health care is a fundamental human right. The number of uninsured has risen by nearly nine million people since 2000. In 2008, United Methodist Women partnered with Healthcare-NOW! to address the health care crisis by supporting a campaign to promote a universal, single-payer health plan in the United States. United Methodist Women members were encouraged to engage their communities and legislators in promoting access to quality, affordable, and accessible health care for all in the following ways:

- Engaging in Healthcare-NOW! audits of local churches, school boards, nonprofits, and local governments to assess the potential budget savings if single-payer health care were enacted and making the findings public
- Working with the Public Policy Office of United Methodist Women to advocate for federal single-payer legislation by encouraging local unit members to contact their representatives
- Working with Healthcare-NOW! and other state coalitions to call on state governments to enact single-payer legislation

Women's Concerns

United Methodist Women members have participated in numerous national phone-in days highlighting the lack of programs addressing women's concerns in the federal budget. Members called for fund transfers from military spending to education, housing, and child health plans, and urged Congress and the president to ratify the United Nations Convention on the Elimination of All Forms of Discrimination Against Women (CEDAW). United Methodist Women has reignited the push for the ratification of CEDAW[7] as well as the implementation of the United Nations Security Council Resolution 1325[8] at the present time.

United Methodist Women members have written letters to express concern about the federal budget cuts affecting human-needs programs and increases in military spending. In March 2003, a United Methodist Women's delegation went to meet with key senators of the Committee on Appropriations, the Budget Committee, and the Committee on Health, Education, Labor, and Pensions. Members pleaded with these senators to support the basic needs and rights of Americans most victimized by budget cuts. They explained that appropriating more money for military spending instead of elementary education would jeopardize the education of children from low-income families. It was clear that without high-quality education, those children would be unable to break the cycle of impoverishment. Likewise, if the budget appropriation of 9 percent for education and training decreased, a student in need of financial assistance would be unable to obtain an advanced degree.

At the United Methodist Women Assembly in 2006 the organization called for a money transfer in the federal budget from military expenditures to money for education and other needed funds for children and youth. In our spring 2007 board meeting, the directors adopted a resolution calling for "Steps toward a Just Peace in the Middle East." We used the United Methodist Social Principles as our guide to affirm that "war is incompatible with the teachings and example of Christ."[9] Through the aftermath of Hurricane Katrina we have seen revealed deep national issues of race and class inequality. United Methodist Women joined with organizations in the rebuilding and reconstruction planning. This effort included raising funds through "Repairers of the Breach," a fund created under the leadership of then United Methodist Women president Kyung Za Yim to assist local units of United Methodist Women in the Gulf region displaced or severely impacted by Hurricanes Katrina and Rita.

Pursuing Justice during the Global Debt Crisis

United Methodist Women joined the worldwide Jubilee movement in the late 1990s and the Jubilee 2000 movement in October 2000 to ensure a collective voice and leadership in the Jubilee and global debt cancellation efforts. Children and women in the global south bear most of the cost of debt repayment. Yet the voices most often heard shaping the discourse on debt are from European or American politicians. Around the world the experiences of poor people are absent from the systems of governance and policymaking such that their priorities and concerns are often filtered. United Methodist Women was one of the first faith-based organizations to endorse the campaign for debt relief of the poorest countries with collection of petition signatures since 1997. The United Methodist Church reconfirmed its commitment to Jubilee 2000 at its General Conference in May 2000.

In April 2004, on the occasion of the sixtieth anniversary of the World Bank and International Monetary Fund (IMF), United Methodist Women engaged in the Unhappy Birthday campaign with Jubilee USA by sending Unhappy Birthday cards to the World Bank calling for debt cancellation of developing countries. The World Bank is the principle financial institution responsible for the crippling debt owed by the developing world. Such debt prevents girls in Africa, Asia, and Latin America from going to school and makes it impossible for poor countries to provide health care and safe drinking water to their citizens. Ten thousand cards from United Methodist Women were sent calling for cancellation of debt for the poorest nations.

In addition, United Methodist Women has continued to support and engage in a national campaign to push for the passage of the Jubilee Act, which calls for cancellation of impoverished-country debt, prohibition of harmful economic policy conditions on debt cancellation, transparency and responsibility in lending from governments and international financial institutions, a new legal framework to restrict the activities of predatory funds, and a U.S. audit of debts resulting from odious and illegitimate lending. During the 1999 G8 meeting in Cologne, Germany, the United States promised to cancel 100 percent of the debt owed to the United States by the eligible countries. Jubilee USA, along with its partners, including United Methodist Women, pressured and negotiated with Congress to make this pledge a reality.

Food Security and Relief for Families

One hundred people of faith, many of them United Methodists, from twenty-six states traveled to the nation's capital on March 2002 to press for policy changes that would help ensure that everyone who can work moves successfully from welfare to employment. The meeting, sponsored by the National Council of Churches, was a mix of Bible study, policy analysis, strategy development, and appointments with members of Congress to share concerns as 1996 welfare policy changes came up for review and reauthorization.

A "Call to Poverty Reduction in the Context of Reauthorization of Temporary Assistance to Needy Families (TANF)" was released during the conference. The call urged Congress to provide more funds for TANF to ensure its ability to act as both a work support program and a safety net for those for whom work is not an option. The call offered ten principles for strengthening U.S. welfare policy:

1. Ensure that poverty reduction is a central goal.
2. Provide sufficient federal and state funding.
3. Acknowledge the dignity of work, eliminate barriers to employment, and provide training and education necessary for unskilled workers to get and hold jobs.
4. Continue and encourage public and private partnerships to train workers and help hold jobs.
5. Allow TANF recipients to retain a substantial portion of wage earnings and assets before becoming ineligible for cash, housing, health, child care, food assistance, or other benefits. Increase funding for the Child Care and Development Block Grant. The food stamp program should be restored for legal immigrants. Outreach should be increased to enroll more children in the Children's Health Insurance Program.
6. Be available for all people in need.
7. Do not impose time limits on people who are complying with the rules of the program.
8. Acknowledge the responsibilities of both parents and government to provide for the well-being of children.
9. Address the needs of individuals with special situations.
10. Uphold and affirm every person's value, whether employed or not.

United Methodist Women has partnered with Bread for the World (BFW) in their "Africa: Hunger to Harvest" campaign for the past decade. BFW has been committed to making Africa the main focus of its international

> When you talk with your members of Congress, don't be afraid to tell them you are here because of your faith and that faith causes you to care about poor people. We as the faith community have something special to say. While statistics are important, we can approach issues from values and not just the numbers.
>
> — Kay Bengston of the Lutheran Office for Governmental Affairs
>
> From National Council of Churches, "Welfare Policies Should Help, Not Hinder New Workers, Faith Bodies Say," March 15, 2002, www.ncccusa.org/news/02news21.html.

> Ruth, a United Methodist with Faith Matters in Greensboro, North Carolina, was one of three persons sharing personal testimony of working with persons moving from welfare to work at a Faith Matters gathering. Ruth told of a thirty-year-old client who is piecing her life together with Medicaid, food stamps, and a fifteen to nineteen hour a week job in a fast-food restaurant. Her "Section 8" subsidized housing allowance covered slightly more than half her rent, and her earnings were inadequate for the balance. "She has a voucher for a six-month certified nursing course, and we are trying to get her a break on housing for six months so she can take the course and get a better paying job," Ruth said.

advocacy for as long as it takes to reverse today's negative trends and to reduce hunger in the continent. For more than thirty-five years, BFW has been a Christian voice for ending hunger and seeking justice.

Today we continue to push for protection of funding for life-saving, poverty-focused foreign assistance with Bread for the World and many other organizations by calling members of Congress and bringing to light how critical their budget decision is to millions of lives around the world.

Along with efforts to shape public policy, United Methodist Women has supported complementary efforts that directly address economic development in developing countries. For example, United Methodist Women has provided assistance to a micro-enterprise minimarket that helps women in East Africa become self-sufficient. Regional Missionary Elmira Sellu has been providing training for women in entrepreneurship so they know how to start a business and how to sustain it.

Sellu explains that the United Methodist women in East Africa are striving for possible ways of turning away from male-dominated traditions. They are raising their voices. Several activities of small and big enterprises are now in full gear. At Nabulagala United Methodist Church in Uganda, women now smile about profits earned from a shop that was set up last year.

The shop sells commodities, mainly food items such as corn flour, millet flour, rice, sugar, salt, cooking oil, and other items for domestic use. Minimarket president Ressa Namaza says the enterprise has registered tremendous growth: "Since April 2010, we are able to earn a profit of 350 U.S. dollars per month. We launched a drive where each member contributes food items for stock during the seasons of plenty. This helps us sell these items at a profitable price during the season of demand. We are also happy that the surrounding communities are supportive. Our products are at high standard, and we have the best customer care."[10]

Hurricane Katrina: A Media Analysis

Right after Hurricane Katrina, the section of Christian Social Responsibility of United Methodist Women's national office worked with the section directors on taking a critical look at how poor areas of Louisiana and neighboring states were being resourced—or not—in the hurricane's aftermath.

We put together an Emergency Response Resource Kit for our members through online research and the assistance of local groups. We also looked at how the federal government was appropriating funds for recovery from Katrina and noted some clear implications of the budgeting process.[11] It was a wake-up call to the continuing need for racial and economic justice work of the Church.

Given all that we learned from an analysis of what transpired in the aftermath of Katrina, United Methodist Women's national office put together a media-monitoring tool to encourage local unit members to evaluate the media critically through the lenses of race, gender, and class. The following is an excerpt from that tool:

> United Methodist Women members are keepers of the vision of a community that is creative and supportive. We also believe in experiencing freedom as whole persons in Jesus Christ. As a faith community, we further believe that all humanity stands as equal in the sight of God who has made us all in God's image. We are God's go-between messengers creating community at the margins. We are God's go-betweens working with the margins. A basic tool for creating community is communication. In order to create community, communication embodies certain functions. It liberates, enhances participation, and brings about just and equitable structures in society. Therefore, as responsible members of faith community, we strive to monitor whether all forms of communication are just, equitable, and participatory. After all, we are engaged in the mission of restoring the image of God in one another.[12]

The following is an illustrative monitoring tool designed to analyze race, gender, and class representation in media coverage:

> **Media monitoring for race and class representation:**
> 1. Date
> 2. Name
> 3. Name of newspaper, television channel, or radio station
> 4. Who owns the newspaper, television channel, or radio station?
> 5. What do you know about the reporter? What is his or her race, class, gender, age?
> 6. How is the subject of the story treated?
> 7. Who is the focus of the news coverage?
> 8. How are these "news subjects" or persons represented?
> 9. What role do these persons play in the story?
> 10. Are these news subjects quoted and/or shown in the photographs?
> 11. Are stereotypes about race, gender, and class represented?
>   a. In language used
>   b. In what was represented visually
>   c. In what was left out

This tool suggests a template for critical analysis of media coverage of any event or issue.

A girl in class at the "House of Hope," a community-based educational training program in Port-au-Prince, Haiti, for children performing domestic work, sponsored by the Ecumenical Foundation for Peace and Justice (FOPJ). *(Paul Jeffrey)*

Historical Work with a Future

United Methodist Women has historically built and supported mission institutions and programs among the poorest people in our nation and the world in order to empower women and children to achieve a better life for themselves and their families. For decades, members of United Methodist Women have studied issues of poverty, racial justice, environmental degradation, and economic justice and have engaged in service and advocacy. We will continue to be advocates for the poorest people of the world. We will continue to ask questions about failing school systems. We will continue to work with grassroots people for racial justice, ensuring that people of color are not pitted against one another as pawns in corporate and political games. We will continue to work for systemic changes that are just and empowering to all God's children.

From a Theology of Scarcity to a Theology of Abundance: Charity to Justice

Our work as a faith community is cut out for us: to heal the brokenness of this world by our walking and working *with* those persons who are poor. The world is not lacking in food and material resources. The problem is the lack of access for the many while some have an overabundance. Charity will not be enough. Justice must reign, and people of faith must come together to build healthy and whole communities.

When she was serving as Women's Division's assistant general secretary of the Section on Christian Social Responsibility, Lois M. Dauway, former interim deputy general secretary, played a major role in the World Council of Churches (WCC). One report she brought to our board of directors regarding the work of WCC was about its engagement in a process called "Project 21," which relates to the United Nation's Millennium Development Goals.[13] She shared the findings of Project 21 titled *Christianity, Poverty and Wealth* by Michael Taylor, director of the World Faiths Development Dialogue and professor of social theology at the University of Birmingham, England. Taylor had found that the teachings of churches around the globe on issues of wealth and poverty could be grouped into four categories: spiritualizing, prosperity, liberation, and holistic.

1. Spiritualizing: Good news to the poor *is* the news of spiritual salvation. It is about church growth through individual conversion. Tackling poverty, especially its structural and political dimensions, is not a spiritual issue. The motives for this spiritualizing approach to poverty promote a form of Christianity full of comfortable hymn singing that supports the status quo and carefully avoids issues of justice and social change.

2. Prosperity: Some see the prosperity gospel, serving the interests of capitalism, being promoted around the world. It is in favor of material blessings but

is opposed to "material" concerns like politics and structural change in favor of justice.

3. Liberation: Bringing good news to the poor in the sense of liberating them from poverty and injustice is not just an aspect of God but a sharply focused, defining characteristic of God, the mission of Jesus, and the task of the churches. If God is on the side of the poor, then, as witnesses to God's kindom, the churches have an unavoidable responsibility to side with the poor as well. In some parts of the world, liberation theology is declining and prosperity theology is growing.

4. Holistic: A both–and theology, which is both spiritual and material. The good news of the gospel is about liberation, both spiritual and material. The church is an institution for both spiritual and material transformation, meaning churches should preach the gospel and at the same time bring development to the communities they serve.[14]

Dauway emphasized the importance of this both–and theology when examining poverty and wealth. There should be "no dichotomy between the sacred and the secular, between Saturday night and Sunday morning in the manner in which we view theology and the manner in which we live out that theology,"[15] she said. She suggested we hold steadfastly to a holistic theology addressing the spiritual and the material. She called on the board of directors and staff to think beyond the charity model of fighting poverty and to also embrace a justice model. Such a model invites the poor to the table of reconciliation, addresses the root causes of poverty, and engages in making systemic changes—all for the sake of the lost and the least and to restore this broken world.

Notes

1. Peggy Johnson, "How to Discern Between Charity and Justice: Means and Ends Are Not the Same," *Faith in Action*, November 10, 2010, www.umc-gbcs.org/site/apps/nlnet/content.aspx?c=frLJK2PKLqF&b=6377065&ct=8863255.

2. Carol Barton, "Systems and Structures that Keep People in Poverty," www.ministrywith.org/learn/systems.html.

3. "Poverty Survey to Assist United Methodist Women in Mission in Their Communities," December 1, 2004, gbgm-umc.org/umw/wdnews.cfm?articleid=2834#%23.

4. Diane Dujon and Ann Withorn, *For Crying Out Loud: Women's Poverty in the United States* (Brooklyn, NY: South End Press, 1996).

5. RUGMARK is the international label against illegal child labor in the carpet industry. Hundreds of the companies around the world have already joined RUGMARK and have made their carpet sourcing child-labor proof.

6. Marian Edelman Wright, e-mail message upon the announcement of President Obama's 2009 SCHIP Reauthorization, February 2009.

7. CEDAW is the international human rights treaty that addresses gender equality, adopted in 1979 by the UN General Assembly, and is often described as an international bill of rights for women.

8. United Nations Security Council Resolution 1325 was adopted unanimously in October 2000. The council called for the adoption of a gender perspective that included the special needs of women and girls during repatriation and resettlement, rehabilitation, reintegration, and postconflict reconstruction.

9. "The World Community: War and Peace," *The Book of Discipline of The United Methodist Church*, 2008 (Nashville: Abingdon Press, 2008), ¶165C.

10. Personal communication, Elmira Sellu, Regional Missionary for United Methodist Women, East Africa Annual Conference.

11. "Katrina and the Federal Budget," *Journal of the Women's Division Fall Meeting 2005*, Women's Division, General Board of Global Ministries, The United Methodist Church, October 2005, 261–263.

12. This statement is based on "Proper Use of Information Communication Technologies," Resolution 8011, *The Book of Resolutions of The United Methodist Church*, 2008 (Nashville: The United Methodist Publishing House, 2008), 934–938.

13. *Journal of the Women's Division Spring Meeting 2005*, Women's Division, General Board of Global Ministries, The United Methodist Church, April 2005, 198–201.

14. Michael Taylor, *Christianity, Poverty and Wealth*, (Geneva: World Council of Churches, 2004).

15. *Journal of the Women's Division Spring Meeting* 2005, 199.

Srey Mao, 14, raises chickens in Khnach, a village in the Kampot region of Cambodia. Along with another sister, she lives with and takes care of her aging grandmother. Her parents died of AIDS. *(Paul Jeffrey)*

Conclusion

So where have we been? What have we seen? How have we felt? And what have we learned?

Denise Johnson Stovall, in Chapter 1, helped us recognize that actually encountering poor people makes a difference. It changes how those who are not poor perceive poor people—they are seen as God sees them, as beloved children of God. Encountering the poor changes how we perceive ourselves. Our previous assumptions about "us" versus "them" begin to break down. And encountering the poor helps all of us begin to experience what it feels like to be members together of a community.

In Chapter 2, we learned that the Bible presents a countercultural vision of our common life, a picture of how things are supposed to be in our communities. The biblical vision makes perfectly clear that God is not neutral about poverty—God finds it abhorrent! Concern for poor people is not an optional add-on feature of our faith. Showing generosity toward the poor and working to establish justice for the poor are essential elements of authentic Christian faith.

In Chapter 3, Kenneth L. Carder helped us recover the Wesleyan roots of concern for the poor. John Wesley was convinced that personally encountering poor people was a crucial aspect of Christian discipleship. Such encounters break down barriers between social classes, cultivate empathy for the poor and downtrodden, create communities in which all are welcome, and, finally, are a means of grace. The love for poor persons that was deepened by personal contact led Wesley to be an advocate for the poor, challenging unjust structures in his society. The same could and should be true for us today.

Pamela D. Couture, in Chapter 4, rightly contended that poverty in the United States is not monolithic; rather, she spoke of poverties, especially as they affect women and children. Having a "macro" picture of poverty in the United States allows us to see the nature and scope of poverty and to assess the relative effectiveness of policy responses. This picture helps us to recognize that some people in our society—reminiscent of the widow, orphans, and resident aliens in the Bible—are especially vulnerable to poverty: children, single-parent families headed by mothers, and Native American, black, and Hispanic persons.

David Wildman's discussion in Chapter 5 makes us realize that advocacy for the global poor requires us to be knowledgeable about the structural biases in the modern global economy. The old adage to "teach someone to fish" has to be extended so that local communities get to eat the fish they catch! Global trade can be a blessing, but only when the terms are such that it serves the needs of local populations in so-called developing nations.

Elizabeth Calvin, in Chapter 6, provided a helpful complement to Chapter 5. Recognizing that women

Young people from Ellensburg, Washington, participate in a demonstration outside the U.S. federal court in Yakima, Washington, to express support for people arrested in a January 20, 2011, immigration sweep in Ellensburg.
(Paul Jeffrey)

throughout our global village struggle because of economic injustice, she proposes practical actions that we can take to help alleviate or eliminate the poverty of women in particular places. Fair trade and microfinance suggest opportunities to work for justice that do not have to wait on policy changes at the national and international levels. We learn what remarkable women have already done and that great things are within our reach.

In Chapter 7, Paul L. Escamilla pointed out that the dominant culture in America values people only to the degree that they are consumers. Our Christian faith suggests that a better descriptive term for who we really are is *companions*. We discover that life in abundance is not a matter of clutching things tightly but of giving and receiving as equal members in community.

In Chapter 8, Sung-ok Lee helped us grasp why addressing the symptoms of poverty with charity is not enough. Working for justice means grappling with the root causes of poverty. She provided multiple illustrations by recounting the highlights of what United Methodist Women has been doing in recent years to "cry out loud"—to band together, organize, strategize, and educate ourselves together to make a difference on behalf of poor people in the United States and throughout the world.

So where do we go from here? What are we going to do? What kind of persons and congregations are we going to be? What are the next steps? What might be the next steps for you? Here are some possibilities:

- Continued personal education: By participating in this mission study you have already begun this step. Keep learning about poverty issues by read-

ing, checking the Ministry with the Poor website (www.ministrywith.org), viewing poverty-related films, and joining small-group studies.
- Leadership: Look for ways that you can lift up poverty issues in your congregation. You can work through United Methodist Women, certainly. Perhaps you could be a member of the social outreach or mission program committee at your congregation. Might you organize or join a committee to address poverty issues in your district or annual conference?
- Direct services: This involves direct action to meet the immediate needs of poor people. Volunteer at a food bank, clothes bank, soup kitchen, shelter for homeless persons, Habitat for Humanity build, or school in an underprivileged neighborhood that needs tutors or visit inmates in a jail or prison.
- Simpler living: Are you ready to make lifestyle changes to reduce your level of consumption? If those changes save you money, devote that savings to ministry with the poor. If you make changes that mean you can work for pay for fewer hours, devote some of those hours saved to ministry with the poor.
- Contribute financially: Mission giving of United Methodist Women supports projects and ministries that address issues of poverty and the needs of women, children, and youth. Besides United Methodist Women gifts to mission, seek out projects funded by both The United Methodist Church as well as those supported by your annual conference. Support other organizations that work to alleviate or eliminate poverty on a local, national, or international level.
- Global solidarity: Get involved in projects that alleviate poverty and build relationships with poor people in other countries to partner together to alleviate poverty.
- Legislative advocacy: Get involved with a group or network working to influence poverty-related public policy at the local, state, or national level.

You will learn only from experience which step is right for you now, and which will be the right next step. Wherever you begin, whatever you do next, remember that "Christ has no body but yours."

Christ Has No Body

Christ has no body but yours,
no hands, no feet on earth but yours.
Yours are the eyes with which he looks
compassion on this world.
Yours are the feet with which he walks to
do good.
Yours are the hands, with which he blesses
all the world.
Yours are the hands, yours are the feet,
yours are the eyes, you are his body.
Christ has no body now but yours,
no hands, no feet on earth but yours.
Yours are the eyes with which he looks
compassion on this world.
Christ has no body now on earth but yours.

— Teresa of Avila (1515–1582)

Silvani Joseph, 48, survived the January 12, 2010, earthquake and carries debris as she and her neighbors begin to build temporary shelters in the Port-au-Prince neighborhood of Belair in Haiti. *(Paul Jeffrey)*

Bibliography

American Sociological Association. "Sociologists Find Lowest-Paid Women Suffer Most from Motherhood Penalty." October 5, 2010. www.asanet.org/press/motherhood_penalty.cfm.

Annie E. Casey Foundation. *Kids Count 2010 Data Book*. Baltimore, MD: Annie E. Casey Foundation. datacenter.kidscount.org/DataBook/2010/OnlineBooks/2010DataBook.pdf.

Barton, Carol. "Systems and Structures that Keep People in Poverty." www.ministrywith.org/learn/systems.html.

Bell, Beverly. "Haitian Farmers Commit to Burning Monsanto Seeds." May 17, 2010. www.otherworldsarepossible.org/another-haiti-possible/haitian-farmers-commit-burning-monsanto-hybrid-seeds.

The Blessing Basket Project. "Founding Story." www.blessingbasket.org/?loc_id=62.

Bloom, Linda. "Women Seek Vital Role in Haiti Recovery." General Board of Global Ministries. http://gbgm-umc.org/global_news/full_article.cfm?articleid=5706.

Bornstein, David, and Susan Davis. *Social Entrepreneurship: What Everyone Needs to Know*. New York: Oxford University Press, 2010.

Buber, Martin. *Paths in Utopia*, translated by R. F. C. Hull. New York: Macmillan, 1950.

Campbell, Ted A. "The Image of Christ in the Poor." In *The Poor and the People Called Methodist*, edited by Richard P. Heitzenrater. Nashville: Kingswood Books, 2002.

Carcaño, Minerva G. *I Believe in Jesus*. New York: Women's Division, The General Board of Global Ministries, The United Methodist Church, 2008.

Children's Defense Fund. *2000 National Observance of Children's Sabbaths Manual*. Washington, DC: Children's Defense Fund, 2000.

The Council of Bishops of The United Methodist Church, *Children and Poverty: An Episcopal Initiative*. Nashville: The United Methodist Publishing House, 1996.

Couture, Pamela D. *Blessed Are the Poor? Women's Poverty, Family Policy, and Practical Theology*. Nashville: Abingdon Press, 1991.

Couture, Pamela D. *Child Poverty: Love, Justice and Social Responsibility*. St. Louis: Chalice Press, 2007.

Crow, Ben, and Suresh K. Lodha. *The Atlas of Global Inequalities*. Berkeley, CA: University of California Press, 2011.

Currie, Janet, and Enrico Morietti. "Biology as Destiny? Short and Long Run Determinants of Birthweight." August 2005. www.econ.ucla.edu/people/papers/currie/more/IGC_aug05.pdf.

Dayton, Donald. "Whither Evangelicalism?" In *Sanctification and Liberation: Liberation Theologies in Light of the Wesleyan Tradition*, edited by Theodore Runyon. Nashville: Abingdon Press, 1981.

Donahue, John R. "Biblical Perspectives on Justice." In *The Faith That Does Justice*, edited by John C. Haughey. New York: Paulist Press, 1977.

Dujon, Diane, and Ann Withorn. *For Crying Out Loud: Women's Poverty in the United States*. Brooklyn, NY: South End Press, 1996.

"The Economic Community: Poverty." *The Book of Discipline of The United Methodist Church, 2008*. Nashville: Abingdon Press, 2008, ¶163E.

Environmental Justice Foundation. *Slave Nation: State-Sponsored Forced Child Labour in Uzbekistan's Cotton Fields*. London: Environmental Justice Foundation, 2009.

Environmental Justice Foundation. *White Gold: Uzbekistan, A Slave Nation for Our Cotton?* London: Environmental Justice Foundation, 2010.

Equal Exchange. "Our Story." www.equalexchange.coop/our-co-op.

Escamilla, Paul. *Longing for Enough in a Culture of More*. Nashville: Abingdon Press, 2007.

Evans, Christopher. *The Kingdom is Always But Coming: A Biography of Walter Rauschenbusch*. Waco, TX: Baylor University Press, 2010.

The General Board of Pension and Health Benefits of the United Methodist Church. "Credit Enhancement and Positive Social Purpose Lending Program." www.gbophb.org/sri_funds/articles/CreditEnhancementPSP.asp.

Greenhalgh, Michelle. "Haitian Farmers Reject Monsanto Donation." *Field Safety News*, June 7, 2010. www.food-safetynews.com/2010/06/haitian-farmers-burn-monsanto-hybrid-seeds.

Hays, Richard B. "You Always Have the Poor with You." *Biblical Literacy Today* 3, no. 2 (Winter 1988–1989).

Heitzenrater, Richard P., ed. *The Poor and the People Called Methodists*. Nashville: Kingwood Books, 2002.

Heitzenrater, Richard P. *Wesley and the People Called Methodists 1729–1999*. Nashville: Abington Press, 1995.

Heschel, Abraham J. *The Prophets*. New York: Harper & Row, 1962.

Hoppe, Leslie J.. *There Shall Be No Poor Among You: Poverty in the Bible*. Nashville: Abingdon Press, 2004.

International Crisis Group. *The Curse of Cotton: Central Asia's Destructive Monoculture*. New York, International Crisis Group, 2005.

International Labor Rights Forum. "Creating a Sweatfree World." www.laborrights.org/creating-a-sweatfree-world.

International Labor Rights Forum. [Homepage.] www.laborrights.org.

International Labour Organization. "Facts on Women at Work." www2.ilo.org/public/english/region/eurpro/budapest/download/womenwork.pdf.

Jacobs, Mary. "Penny Project Nets Big Bucks." *United Methodist Reporter*, July 18, 2008. www.umportal.org/article.asp?id=3835.

Jefferson, Thomas. *Thomas Jefferson: Writings*. New York: Literary Classics of the United States, 1984.

Jennings, Theodore W. *Good News to the Poor: John Wesley's Evangelical Economics*. Nashville: Abingdon Press, 1990.

Johnson, Peggy. "How to Discern Between Charity and Justice: Means and Ends Are Not the Same." *Faith in Action*, November 10, 2010. www.umc-gbcs.org/site/apps/nlnet/content.aspx?c=frLJK2PKLqF&b=6377065&ct=8863255.

Kaplan, Joan. "Penny Project Uses Pocket Change to Enact Change." United Methodist News Service, December 10, 2008. www.umc.org/site/apps/nlnet/content3.aspx?c=lwL4KnN1LtH&b=2429867&ct=6441973.

"Katrina and the Federal Budget." *United Methodist Women Journal*, October 2005, 261–263.

Kidder, Tracy. *Mountains Beyond Mountains*. New York: Random House, 2003.

Lappé, Anna. "Who Says Food is a Human Right?" *The Nation*, October 3, 2011.

Lebow, Victor, "Price Competition in 1955." *Journal of Retailing* (Spring 1955).

Leistikow, Nicole. "Women Gain Inch in Push for Land Rights in Uganda." Women eNews, July 20, 2003. www.womensenews.org/story/the-world/030720/women-gain-inch-push-land-rights-uganda.

Long, Thomas G. *Matthew: Westminster Bible Companion*. Louisville: Westminster John Knox, 1997.

Luther, Martin. *Luther's Works*. Vol. 45. Philadelphia, Fortress Press, 1962.

Magnusen, Karen A., and Sharon M. McGroder, "The Effect of Increasing Welfare Mothers' Education on their Young Children's Academic Problems and School Readiness." Joint Center for Poverty Research at Northwestern University and University of Chicago. www.northwestern.edu/ipr/jcpr/workingpapers/wpfiles/magnuson_mcgroder.pdf.

Martin, Roger L., and Sally Osberg. "Social Entrepreneurship: The Case for Definition." *Stanford Social Innovation Review* (Spring 2007).

Mason, Jason. "Assisting the Poor: Assistance Programmes in the Bible." *Transformation* (April–June 1987): 1–14.

McCann, J. Clinton. "The Book of Psalms: Introduction, Commentary, and Reflections." In *The New Interpreter's Bible*. Vol. 4, edited by Leander E. Keck. Nashville: Abingdon Press, 1996.

Meeks, M. Douglas, ed. *The Portion of the Poor*. Nashville: Kingswood Books, 1995.

Michigan in Brief. "Welfare Reform: TANF Reauthorization." www.michiganinbrief.org/edition07/Chapter5/WelformReform.htm.

Miller, Patrick D. *Deuteronomy. Interpretation: A Bible Commentary for Teaching and Preaching*. Louisville, KY: John Knox, 1990.

Ministry with the Poor Guiding Principles and Foundations: Answering Jesus' Call to Discipleship in God's Mission of Love and Justice. Interagency Task Force on Ministry with the Poor, The United Methodist Church, October 29, 2010. http://new.gbgm-umc.org/media/pdf/110209dlwithprinciples.pdf.

Minsky, Tequila. "A Tribute." **response** 43, no. 5 (May 2011): 31–33.

Mott, Stephen, and Ronald J. Sider, "Economic Justice: A Biblical Paradigm." In *Toward a Just and Caring Society: Christian Responses to Poverty in America*, edited by David P. Gushee. Grand Rapids: Baker Books, 1999.

Nabakov, Vladmir. *Pale Fire*. Lancer Books, 1989.

National Poverty Center. "Poverty in the United States, Frequently Asked Questions." The National Poverty Center, University of Michigan, www.npc.umich.edu/poverty/#3.

"The Nature, Design, and General Rules of Our United Societies." *The Book of Discipline of The United Methodist Church*, 2008. Nashville: Abingdon Press, 2008, ¶103.

Nest, Michael. *Coltan*. Cambridge: Polity Press, 2011.

The Network of NGOs of Trinidad and Tobago for the Advancement of Women. "The Women's Responsive Sou Sou Banking System." www.networkngott.org/index.php?option=com_content&view=article&id=12&Itemid=17.

"The Nobel Peace Prize 2006: Muhammad Yunus, Grameen Bank." www.nobelprize.org/nobel_prizes/peace/laureates/2006.

Nussbaum, Martha C. *Women and Human Development: The Capabilities Approach*. Cambridge: Cambridge University Press, 2000.

Opportunity International. "Rosemary Namande." www.opportunity.org/media-center/videos/rosemary-namande/#.TtOzaWDK3Hk.

Opportunity International. "Women's Opportunity Network." www.opportunity.org/womens-opportunity-network/#.TtOzxWDK3Hk.

Pankow, Debra. "How Much Should We Spend?" North Dakota State University. Revised June 2009. www.ag.ndsu.edu/pubs/yf/fammgmt/fe440w.htm.

Partners for Just Trade. "About Partners for Just Trade." www.partnersforjusttrade.org/ht/d/sp/i/179/pid/179.

Pearce, Diana. "The Feminization of Poverty: Women, Work, and Welfare." *Urban and Social Change Review* 11 (1978): 28–36.

Pogge, Thomas. *Politics as Usual: What Lies Behind the Pro-Poor Rhetoric*. Cambridge: Polity Press, 2010.

"Poverty Survey to Assist United Methodist Women in Mission in Their Communities." December 1, 2004. gbgm-umc.org/umw/wdnews.cfm?articleid=2834#%23.

"Proper Use of Information Communication Technologies." Resolution 8011. *The Book of Resolutions of The United Methodist Church*, 2008. Nashville: The United Methodist Publishing House, 2008.

Pryor, Donald. "Access to Subsidized Child Care in Monroe County, New York." Center for Governmental Research, September 2007. www.cgr.org/reports/07_R-1524_AccesstoSubsidizedChildCareinMC.pdf.

Richey, Russell E., Kenneth E. Rowe, and Jean Miller Schmidt. *The Methodist Experience in America: A History*. Vol. 1. Nashville: Abingdon Press, 2010.

Robert, Dana L. *Joy to the World: Mission in the Age of Global Christianity, A Mission Study for 2010 and 2011*. New York: Women's Division, The General Board of Global Ministries, The United Methodist Church, 2010.

Sabour, Azadeh, and Matthew Barg. "Complicity in the Congo." Sustainalytics webinar, November 23, 2010. www.sustainalytics.com/conflict-minerals-complicity-congo.

SERRV. "Artisan Stories." www.serrv.org/category/artisan-stories.

Shah, Anup. "Poverty Facts and Stats." Global Issues. Updated September 20, 2001. www.globalissues.org.

Skocpol, Theda. *Protecting Soldiers and Mothers: The Political Origins of Social Policy in the United States*. Boston: Belknap Press, 1992.

Smith, Phil, and Eric Thurman. *A Billion Bootstraps—Microcredit, Barefoot Banking and the Business Solution for Ending Poverty*. New York: McGraw Hill, 2007.

Tanton, Tim. "Fighting Poverty with Jam." United Methodist News Service, July 23, 2009. www.umc.org/site/apps/nlnet/content3.aspx?c=lwL4KnN1LtH&b=5259669&ct=7237963.

Taylor, Michael. *Christianity, Poverty and Wealth*. Geneva: World Council of Churches, 2004.

Ten Thousand Villages. "Our History: Roots of a Global Movement." www.tenthousandvillages.com/php/about.us/about.history.php.

Thompson, Francis. "The Kingdom of God." In *The Oxford Book of English and Mystical Verse*, edited by D. H. S. Nicholson and A. H. E. Lee. Oxford: Clarendon Press, 1917.

UNICEF. "Child Mortality Rate Drops by a Third Since 1990." September 16, 2010. www.unicefusa.org/news/releases/child-mortality-rate-drops.html.

UNICEF. "Gender Equality: The Big Picture." Updated August 25, 2004. www.unicef.org/gender/index_bigpicture.html.

U.S. Bureau of Labor Statistics. "Median Weekly Earnings for Men and Women in Fourth Quarter 2010." www.bls.gov/opub/ted/2011/ted_20110124.htm.

U.S. Department of Agriculture, Economic Research Service. "Food CPI and Expenditures, Table 7." Updated July 13, 2011. www.ers.usda.gov/Briefing/CPIFoodAndExpenditures/Data/Expenditures_tables/table7.htm.

Ward, W. Reginald, and Richard P. Heitzenrater, eds. *The Works of John Wesley*. Vol. 18, *Journals and Diaries I*. Nashville: Abingdon Press, 1988.

Ward, W. Reginald, and Richard P. Heitzenrater, eds. *The Works of John Wesley*. Vol. 20: *Journals and Diaries III, 1743–54*. Nashville: Abingdon Press, 1991.

Ward, W. Reginald, and Richard P. Heitzenrater, eds. *The Works of John Wesley*. Vol. 21: *Journals and Diaries IV, 1755–65*. Nashville: Abingdon Press, 1992.

Ward, W. Reginald, and Richard P. Heitzenrater, eds. *The Works of John Wesley*. Vol. 23. Nashville: Abingdon Press, 1995.

Weitzman, Lenore J. *The Divorce Revolution: The Unexpected Social and Economic Consequences for Women and Children in America*. New York: The Free Press, 1985.

Wesley, John. "The Appeals to Men of Reason and Religion." In *The Works of John Wesley*. Vol. 11, edited by Gerald R. Cragg. Nashville: Abingdon Press, 1989.

Wesley, John. "The New Creation." In *The Works of John Wesley*. Vol. 2: *Sermons II*, edited by Albert C. Outler. Nashville: Abingdon Press, 1985.

Wesley, John, "Upon Our Lord's Sermon on the Mount." Discourse IV, Sermon 24. In *John Wesley's Sermons: An Anthology*, edited by Albert C. Outler and Richard P. Heitzenrater. Nashville: Abingdon Press, 2008.

Wesley, John. "The Signs of the Times." In *The Works of John Wesley*. Vol. 2, *Sermons II*, edited by Albert C. Outler. Nashville: Abingdon Press, 1985.

Wesley, John. "Thoughts upon Methodism." In *The Works of John Wesley*. Vol. 9, *The Methodist Societies: History, Nature, and Design*, edited by Rupert E. Davies. Nashville: Abingdon Press, 1989.

Wesley, John. "Thoughts on the Present Scarcity of Provisions." In *The Works of John Wesley*. Vol. 11, Jackson edition. Grand Rapids: Baker Book House, 1979.

Wesley, John. "The Use of Money." In *The Works of John Wesley*. Vol. 2: *Sermons II*, edited by Albert C. Outler. Nashville; Abingdon Press, 1985.

Wesley, John. "On Visiting the Sick." In *The Works of John Wesley*. Vol. 3: *Sermons III*, edited by Albert C. Outler. Nashville: Abingdon Press, 1986.

Wesley, John, and Charles Wesley. *Hymns and Sacred Poems.* London: William Strahan, 1739.

Wildman, David, and Phyllis Bennis. *Ending the War in Afghanistan: A Primer.* Northampton, MA: Olive Branch Press, 2010.

Women's World Banking. "Adisue Ayu: Client of PEACE MFI." www.swwb.org/clients/adisue-ayu-client-peace-mfi.

"The World Community: War and Peace." *The Book of Discipline of The United Methodist Church*, 2008. Nashville: Abingdon Press, 2008, ¶165C.

Yunus, Muhammad. *Banker to the Poor.* New York: Public Affairs, 1999, 2003.

Yunus, Muhammad. *Building Social Business.* New York: Public Affairs, 2010.

Yunus, Muhammad. *Creating a World Without Poverty.* New York: Public Affairs, 2007.

About the Editor

Jack A. Keller Jr. served as project director for the critically acclaimed and best-selling *New Interpreter's Bible* commentary series. Currently co-editor of the 26-volume *Immersion Bible Studies* series, he has been writing and editing resources for laity, pastors, scholars, and students for more than twenty-five years. He holds a PhD in religious ethics from Vanderbilt University.

Contributors

Elizabeth Calvin is a global educator and workshop facilitator, working internationally for more than twenty years in activist grant-making. She advocates for women and children's rights, justice issues, and the basic human right to education, health, food, land, water, housing, and freedom from exploitation. Calvin was a program executive for the General Board of Global Ministries of The United Methodist Church, including Women's Division, and most recently was executive director of the ecumenical World Day of Prayer in the United States.

Kenneth L. Carder is the Ruth W. & A. Morris Williams Jr. Professor Emeritus of the Practice of Christian Ministry and bishop in residence at Duke Divinity School. Previously he served as bishop of the Mississippi and Nashville episcopal areas of The United Methodist Church. He is the author of several books, including *Grace to Lead: Practicing Leadership in the Wesleyan Tradition* (with Laceye C. Warner) and *Living Our Beliefs: The United Methodist Way*.

Pamela D. Couture holds the Jane & Geoffrey Martin Chair in Church and Community in the Emmanuel College of Victoria University at the University of Toronto. Her publications include *Child Poverty: Love, Justice, and Responsibility; Seeing Children, Seeing God: A Practical Theology of Children and Poverty;* and *Blessed Are the Poor? Women's Poverty, Family Policy, and Practical Theology.*

Paul L. Escamilla is senior pastor of Saint John's United Methodist Church in Austin, Texas. He is the author of *True When Whispered: Hearing God's Voice in a Noisy World* and *Longing for Enough in a Culture of More*.

Denise Johnson Stovall of Dallas, Texas, has traveled to Brazil, Puerto Rico, Mexico, eight countries in Africa, and throughout the United States writing stories on the poor. She has been president of seven units of United Methodist Women where her husband, the Rev. L. Charles Stovall, served as a pastor. They have two adult children, Leonard and Deanna.

Sung-ok Lee, a deaconess in The United Methodist Church, is assistant general secretary of Christian social action in the national office of United Methodist Women in New York City.

David Wildman is staff of the United Methodist General Board of Global Ministries where he serves as the executive secretary for justice and discipleship.

Notes